MW00990365

MACHIAVELLI'S
THE
PRINCE

A BEGINNER'S GUIDE

GEORGE MYERSON

Hodder & Stoughton

A MEMBER OF THE HODDER HEADLINE GROUP

Orders: please contact Bookpoint Ltd, 130 Milton Park, Abingdon, Oxon OX14 4SB. Telephone: (44) 01235 827720, Fax: (44) 01235 400454. Lines are open from 9.00–6.00, Monday to Saturday, with a 24-hour message answering service. Email address: orders@bookpoint.co.uk

British Library Cataloguing in Publication Data
A catalogue record for this title is available from The British Library.

ISBN 0 340 84650 X

First published 2002
Impression number   10 9 8 7 6 5 4 3 2 1
Year   2007 2006 2005 2004 2003 2002

Cover design by Mike Stones
Typeset by Transet Limited, Coventry, England.
Printed in Great Britain for Hodder & Stoughton Educational, a division of Hodder Headline Plc, 338 Euston Road, London NW1 3BH by Cox & Wyman, Reading, Berks.

CONTENTS

FOREWORD

Welcome to …

Hodder & Stoughton's Beginner's Guides to Great Works
… your window into the world of the big ideas!

This series brings home for you the classics of western and world thought. These are the guides to the books everyone wants to have read – the greatest moments in science and philosophy, theology and psychology, politics and history. Even in the age of the Internet, these are the books that keep their lasting appeal. As so much becomes ephemeral – the text message, the e-mail, the season's hit that is forgotten in a few weeks – we have a deeper need of something more lasting. These are the books that connect the ages, shining the light of the past on the changing present and expanding the horizons of the future.

However, the great works are not always the most immediately accessible. Though they speak to us directly, in flashes, they are also expressions of human experience and perceptions at its most complex. The purpose of these guides is to take you into the world of these books, so that they can speak directly to your experience.

WHAT COUNTS AS A GREAT WORK?

There is no fixed list of great works. Our aim is to offer as comprehensive and varied a selection as possible from among the books which include:

* **The key points of influence** on science, ethics, religious beliefs, political values, psychological understanding.

* The finest achievements of **the greatest authors**.

* The origins and climaxes in **the great movements** of thought and belief.

* The most provocative arguments, which have aroused **the strongest reactions**, including the most notorious as well as the most praised works.

* The high points of **intellectual style**, wit and persuasion.

READING THIS GUIDE
There are many ways to enjoy this book – whether you are thinking of reading the great work, have tried and want some support or have enjoyed it and want some help to clarify and express your reactions.

These guides will help you appreciate your chosen book if you are taking a course or if you are following your own pathway.

What this guide offers
Each guide aims:

* To tell the whole story of the book, from its origins to its influence.

* To follow the book's argument in a careful and lively way.

* To explain the key terms and concepts.

* To bring in accessible examples.

* To provide further reading and wider questions to explore.

How to approach this guide
These guides are designed to be a coherent read, keeping you turning the pages from start to finish – maybe even in a sitting or two!

At the same time, the guide is also a reference work that you can consult repeatedly as you read the great work or after finishing a passage. To make both reading and consulting easy, the guides have:

* Key quotations with page references to different editions.

* Explanations of key quotes.

Our everyday life is buzzing with messages that get shorter and more disposable every month. Through this guide, you can enter a more lasting dialogue of ideas.

George Myerson
Series Editor

A GREAT WORK

Machiavelli's *The Prince* is a unique combination of elements rarely found together in the history of western thought:

* rigorously argued political *theory*, in which each concept is carefully defined and beautifully linked to every other concept
* acute – and often dramatic – *observation* of specific political actors and events.

The interweaving of theory with narrative, of concept with characterization gives *The Prince* a texture like few other books on politics, power or ethics in general. At once speculative and specific, Machiavelli's *The Prince* formulates *general rules of political life* that we can still draw upon to illuminate the events and the actors of later political times, including our own.

But is there also a corrosive *cynicism* at the heart of this otherwise enlightening work? Generation by generation, readers have been called upon to answer this question – as we are now. To engage with *The Prince* is to participate in one of the longest – and most intense – debates that have shaped modern political thought.

KEY FEATURES

In order to bring out the continuing force of Machiavelli's unique form of argument, this guide includes a number of specific features.

There is a running series of chapter boxes which – together with related sub-headings – will enable you to follow the movement through the logic of *The Prince* section by section. This structure can be used to complement any of the main editions of the work.

A very small number of brief key quotes are given, together with supporting analysis or 'anatomy' of their main points.

Key concepts are briefly picked out and defined.

Machiavelli's main ideas are made immediate, memorable and accessible by being summarized as 'Machiavellian Rules' (or guidelines) using a clear box format for ease of reference.

Finally, modern-day examples are provided to extend and sharpen the explanation of the arguments – and to open up space for further debate!

A NOTE ON EDITIONS

There are a number of easily available modern translations of *The Prince* and this guide is structured so as to complement any of them – following as it does the essential structure of the arguments. The chapter headings – and occasional brief quotes – are as given in the translation by Robert M. Adams (Norton critical edition, 1992), which also has the benefit of an excellent selection of critical texts. Other editions that you might use include those from Penguin Classics (new edition) and Everyman.

INTRODUCTION

AIMS

Generations have been fascinated, appalled and enlightened by this work of political theory and observation written by Niccolo Machiavelli in Florence in 1513.

In this guide we will see:

* Why Machiavelli's *observations of power* and the state still apply – why reading *The Prince* so likely to illuminate current situations in politics, in news.

* How there is a coherent and lasting Machiavellian psychology, a *pragmatic psychology*. *The Prince* is the great work of a uniquely 'non-moralistic' psychologist. Most psychology has a moral bias or twist, but Machiavelli is genuinely interested in human motives and reactions, without needing to make moral judgements.

* What is meant by *Machiavellian realism*: Machiavelli is the great realist, but in the sense that there are realist novelists. His realism is a way of telling stories, of asking questions about character and plot.

REPUTATIONS

The Prince *has evidently excited the interest and admiration of some of the most formidable men of action of the last four centuries, especially our own, men not normally addicted to reading classical texts.*
(Isaiah Berlin, 'The question of Machiavelli')

The Prince is the most notorious of classics, reputed to be the textbook of dictators and yet also a key source for modern political philosophy. On the one hand, there has been the complex history known, mainly by its enemies, as 'Machiavellianism': a byword for political cynicism and treachery. Yet throughout the centuries, Machiavelli has remained a key reference point for some of the leading political theorists in western thought, including Spinoza, Rousseau, Hegel and Gramsci.

There is another duality too. Berlin puts this problem for us. Here is a book that remains 'lucid, succinct and pungent', yet *The Prince* is also baffling in the 'sheer number of interpretations' to which it has given rise: 'There is evidently something peculiarly disturbing about what Machiavelli said or implied.'

In our reading, we will see that Niccolo Machiavelli's *The Prince* is a book about powerful men and their worlds, a unique blend of contemporary detail, theoretical reflection, advice and criticism. Through every page, a balance holds, between massive individuals – Cesare Borgia, Darius, kings of France and Spain, Pope Leo – and their societies, their historic circumstances. There has never been a more integrated vision of the human condition as a fabric woven of individuality and belonging, of free choice and unavoidable circumstance. Together with its notorious violence and potential cynicism, *The Prince*, we will see, is a delicate reflection on how people live in worlds filled with the desires of others, how at our most secret we are often closest to the heart of a dangerously shared circumstance.

Ultimately, all texts are what their interpreters have made of them. This general principle applies with particular force to Machiavelli's *The Prince*, a book whose wisdom lies in being uniquely open to the world. The model for the present reading is a long-standing approach going back at least to the great English historian Clarendon, in the seventeenth century. He drew upon Machiavelli in an attempt to find a method for understanding the violence, and the ambiguity, of his own day:

Machiavell was in the right, though he got an ill name by it with those who take what he said from the report of other men, or do not enough consider themselves what he says, and his method in speaking.

(Clarendon, *History of the Rebellion*, X, pp. 169–70, in Raab, *The English Face of Machiavelli*, p. 152)

Being from a later time, we will not commit ourselves to declaring Machiavelli 'in the right', but we will explore how richly his concepts, understood in particular ways, can still illuminate the dark world.

The contexts of *The Prince*

AIMS

In this chapter, we relate the continuing relevance of *The Prince* to its original context. We see that this is not a book that has attained subsequent influence by being 'ahead of its time'. On the contrary, we see how Machiavelli's great work expresses its time and evolves from a particular life experience in that era. It is because Machiavelli engaged so precisely with his particular circumstances that he continues to provide us with a model of practical reasoning. The intensity of its immersion in its circumstance is what makes *The Prince* talk to other generations in their changing situations.

MACHIAVELLI'S LIFE AND CAREER

Origins

Niccolo was born on 3 May 1469, son of Bernardo di Niccolo di Buoninsegna and his wife Bartolomea de' Nelli. They were socially of the impoverished nobility. His father had a law degree and worked as Secretary for the Florentine republic, but, equally important, he was a noted scholar and humanist. Under his influence, as a child, Machiavelli read widely, notably in ancient philosophy and history. He thus came from an educated, cultured context and also from a political background.

Political background and career

In Florence, from 1434, the famous Medici family was in power, in a reign founded by Cosimo de' Medici. But in 1469, the great Piero died and left two sons, Lorenzo and Giuliano, both young men. A time of violence followed. In 1478, the conspiracy of the Pazzi was brutally suppressed; from 1489 came the rise of Savonarola, the revolutionary and prophetic friar. In 1491 he denounced the ruling Lorenzo the Magnificent. By now Machiavelli was in his twenties,

reaching adulthood in an age of increasing instability. In 1492 Lorenzo
the Magnificent died and in 1494 Charles VIII of France invaded Italy,
claiming Naples. Now the weaker Piero de' Medici was in charge. He
fled and thus ended for the moment the Medici regime in Florence.

Now comes Machiavelli's active phase in politics and diplomacy. His
career belongs to a specific period defined by the historian Pocock as
'the Machiavellian moment':

> *In 1494, Medicean rule collapsed at the advent of the*
> *French army, and toward the end of the year was set up the*
> *constitution that was to symbolise Florentine republicanism*
> *for the brief remainder of its political existence – from 1494*
> *to 1512 and from 1527 to 1530.*
>
> (Pocock, *The Machiavellian Moment*, p. 103)

The French King Charles VIII entered Florence on 17 November
1494. In the aftermath, there emerged a new republic – with a Great
Council, led by Paoloantonio Soderini set up in 1494. This was also
the period of the influence of Savonarola, until his execution in
1498. On 28 May 1498, four days after that execution, Niccolo
Machiavelli, not then well known, was appointed 'Secretary of the
Second Chancery' – being responsible for foreign affairs. The
appointment was confirmed on 19 June 1498 (Viroli, *Niccolo's Smile*,
p. 28).

His general role was to negotiate a way among the conflicts of great
powers for Florence. The context was one of increasing instability. In
1499 there was a new French king, Louis XII – who features as
paradigm of failure in *The Prince*. By 1499, Machiavelli was urging
the Florentines (*ibid.*, p. 40) to reconquer Pisa, to take active risks. In
this phase, Florence executed their own great mercenary leader
Vitelli, a man doomed by his own successes – an incident that
features strongly in the book. Meanwhile, in August 1501
Machiavelli married Marietta Corsini, a relationship that lasted
despite his notorious infidelities.

In 1501 Machiavelli the diplomat begins the encounter with the infamous Cesare Borgia, 'Duke Valentino' who (*ibid.*, p. 52) had taken Rimini and Pesaro and also was stirring up trouble against Florence in other regions. This man was the greatest threat to the safety of the Florentine republic. Borgia was the son of the powerful Pope Alexander VI and was establishing himself, with his father's help, as a power in Italy, taking control of the rich Romagna region. He is to be the key character study at the heart of *The Prince*. On 8 and 9 October 1502, as a leading Florentine diplomat Machiavelli met Cesare Borgia. In his letters, he records his admiring amazement as Borgia describes his powerful enemies as a 'congress of losers'. Machiavelli says that he replied: 'I had always thought of him as the winner.'

---

13 November 1502
'I am dealing with a prince who manages things for himself'
'This lord is very secretive'

26th December 1502
'Messer Ramiro this morning was found in two pieces on the public square, where he still is; and all the people have been able to see him. Nobody feels sure of the cause of his death, except that it has pleased the prince …'

(Viroli, p. 62)

In the aftermath of these encounters, as the region splintered further, Machiavelli took responsibility for the military defence of the state, another key strand in *The Prince*. In 1504 he was setting up a citizens' militia.

There ensued an experience of brutal failure and defeat, the immediate context for *The* Prince. On 26 July 1510 Pope Julius II made a disastrous alliance with Venice against France. In his letters, Machiavelli saw trouble brewing. 'All are disappointed at this move by the pope, who seems to be trying to ruin Christendom and lay the foundations for the destruction of Italy.' In 1510 Machiavelli was back trying to negotiate with the King of France. Conflict between France and the papacy was spreading throughout Italian territories.

In 1511, there emerged a Holy League, an alliance made by the Pope with Venice, Ferrara and Spanish King Ferdinand of Aragon. This League achieved its victory in 1512 against King Louis, but that also signalled disaster for Florence, towards which the Pope was not well disposed. The Florentine regime was crumbling. Spanish troops, allied to the Pope, were outside the city walls.

Florence massed its defences (Viroli, p. 128): 350 horsemen in the city, heavily armed, with 500 more lightly, specifically gathered by Machiavelli, and 14,000 infantry. The Florentine town of Prato was under immediate threat by the Spanish army – it was garrisoned by 3000 infantry. The authorities imprisoned the Medici faction. But on 16 September 1512 there came the sack of Prato by the Spanish army. Machiavelli wrote that 'better than four thousand men died there, and the rest were taken prisoner ... nor did they spare' – Spain defeats the Florentine militia (*ibid.*, p. 129). As Mark Hulliung (p. 62) notes, this confirmed a key theme of Machiavelli's political thought: 'Weak, vacillating, indecisive leadership had marked, so Machiavelli believed, the Florentine republic of 1494 to 1512.'

The time of *The Prince*

On 16 September 1512, Medici supporters gathered in Florence; on 18 September, the republican regime ended; on 7 November 1512 Machiavelli was sacked as Secretary. The Medici came back to power in the city and soon after Giovanni, Cardinal de' Medici was made Pope Leo X in Rome.

Meanwhile, a plot was exposed, a conspiracy against the Medici – and Machiavelli's name was found on a list of allies. He was sent to prison where he stayed for 22 days under torture in February and March 1513. Machiavelli was released on 11 or 12 March 1513, as part of the celebrations for the coronation of the Medici pope. After this terrible period in prison, Machiavelli settled on his farm, but remained desperate to re-enter public life. Here arises a common version of the 'motives' for *The Prince*: that Machiavelli wrote his book to impress the new rulers, Lorenzo de' Medici and specifically the Medici pope who had just come to power in Rome. He was looking for a job, as an adviser, and so was trying to demonstrate both his expertise and the value of such advice more generally, as Quentin Skinner shows.

There was also a more intimate context. Machiavelli disclosed the existence of his book to a close friend, Francesco Vettori, as part of a sustained correspondence through the year 1513. Vettori was employed by the new Florentine state as their representative in Rome at the court of the new pope.

In a letter of 10 December 1513, Machiavelli refers to having composed a 'A short study', some jottings. Machiavelli hopes it can be presented at court. But in a more profound sense, the composition of *The Prince* is woven into the dialogue with Vettori through that year and it is worth focusing briefly on that conversation to understand further the intellectual and even the emotional motives behind the great work. Indeed John M. Najemy has even shown that we could see *The Prince* as 'addressed to Vettori', so interwoven is the work into this personal dialogue.

The dialogue begins with a moment of bitter loneliness, far beyond 'normal' isolation:

> Florence, 13 March 1513, Machiavelli to 'the Magnificent Francesco Vettori, Most worthy Florentine ambassador to the supreme pontiff'
>
> 'Magnificent one. As you must have learnt ... I got out of prison, amid this city's universal rejoicing ...'

This is the beginning of the immediate moment of *The Prince*.

In his letter, Machiavelli immediately acknowledges the dominant feeling of isolation, not anger, not envy, but shame:

> 'I shall not repeat the long story of my disgrace.'

As the dialogue unfolds, Machiavelli can be heard saying that he feels better – better about himself in the first instance. I have had troubles, he says, and:

> Machiavelli, 18 March 1513
> 'I have borne them so straightforwardly that I am proud of myself for it and consider myself more of a man than I believed I was.'

This is a touching sentence and also a psychologically profound one. In the first letter, we have the pure outsider, alone in the happy world. His own history had become a long story of disgrace – a matter of shame. Now his self-esteem returns and it is in this process that *The Prince* is conceived and written.

In their letters, Machiavelli and Vettori begin more and more to discuss current political events and the characters that feature in *The Prince*. Vettori tends to be wary of Machiavelli's enthusiasm for rational explanations and theories. Machiavelli has to defend his need to make sense of events so systematically. On 30 March 1513, Machiavelli expresses, or even confesses, that he is possessed by an overwhelming need to discuss politics: 'Because Fortune has seen to it that since I do not know how to talk about either the silk or the wool trade, or profits and losses, I have to talk about politics. I need either to take a vow of silence or to discuss this' (Viroli, p. 144). His correspondent was not always willing to go along with this conversation. Machiavelli sometimes seems to his more mundane friend to be carried away and so he has to defend his intense passion for analysis.

There is a famous letter of 10 December 1513, which begins by picturing his circumstances:

I am living on my farm.

I make my way along the road toward the inn, I chat with passers-by.

(Cited in Viroli, p. 150ff and reprinted in the edition of the letters, **Between Friends**)

Machiavelli then describes his experience of writing the book, a description that is uniquely intimate for the genesis of such an ancient work:

> 'When evening comes, I return home and enter my study; on the threshold, I take off my workday clothes, covered with mud and dirt, and put on the garments of court and palace. Fitted out appropriately, I step inside the venerable courts of the ancients ... where I am unashamed to converse with them ...'

The reply was offhand. On 24 December 1513, Vettori: responded briefly: 'You write to me ... that you have composed a work about states.' In fact, Machiavelli's practical plan did not succeed – his work did not win him favour. He lamented: 'So I am going to stay just as I am, amid my lice.'

Machiavelli's later years

But eventually, Machiavelli re-entered social life. During 1517 he joined a new group meeting in the Orti Oricellari, palazzo of Bernardo Rucellai. In 1517–19 he composed two successful comedies *Andria* and *The Mandrake*. To these years belongs the composition of *The Discourses*. This was a book on the Roman republic as presented by the classical historian Livy. Its theme was the success of republics and, specifically, how the Roman republic stayed free. It needs to be noted here that there has long been controversy about the chronological sequence of Machiavelli's thought (Hulliung,

p. 233). On one side, there is the thesis of Chabod that the conception of *The Discourses* actually pre-dates the writing of *The Prince* – and on the other, the later orthodoxy, via Hans Baron, that, as in this account, *The Prince* is the first step. The current view tends to downplay the significance of the ordering.

In 1519 Lorenzo de' Medici died. Now Machiavelli was employed again by the Florentine Signoria and sent to Luca on a diplomatic mission. He wrote a number of other works:

* 1520 *Summary of the Civic Affairs of Luca.*

* 1520 *Life of Castruccio Castracani.*

* 1521 *Discourse on Florentine Affairs After the Death of Lorenzo.*

* 1521 *The Art of War.*

Through the early 1520s, he was working on *The Florentine Histories*, completed in early March 1525 for Giulio Cardinal de' Medici, by now Pope Clement VII.

On 21 June 1527, just before his death, Machiavelli declared he dreamt that he had refused to enter heaven, insisting he would be better in hell, with the other politicians of his time.

THE INTELLECTUAL BACKGROUND
We now turn to the play of ideas against which *The Prince* came to life. The book's original moment is one where a number of different political traditions overlapped and collided. The key is an overlapping of different 'discourses'.

'The New Political Theory' of the early Renaissance
In the period immediately before *The Prince*, a new approach to politics began to appear, typified by Sir John Fortescue's 'In Praise of the Laws of England' (1468–71). As Pocock summarizes (p. 23), the key question was: 'What sort of knowledge is possible of the particular?'

Felix Raab (p. 22) notes that the work of Fortescue and others is an important precursor of Machiavelli in the negative sense of separating the issue of the state from theology – where it had rested in medieval theory – though not yet breaking through into the specific concept of an autonomous field of politics. Here we have 'the language of men talking about the affairs of *this* world'.

Florentine traditions

There were a number of specifically Florentine traditions. **Dante** and earlier fourteenth-century Florence evolved a political theory of empire (Pocock, pp. 52–3): 'Affiliation with the empire, then, like affiliation with monarchy generally, was affiliation with the timeless.' Empire was a continuing theme in Machiavelli, as noted by Hulliung. From Dante, there also came a concern with fortune and how to overcome its, or her, influence, as charted by Hannah Pitkin.

But alongside, there was the theory of rhetoric associated with **Petrarch**. This tradition was about practical communication: 'The humanist stress on communication was enough to raise the question of how particular men, existing at particular moments, could lay claim to secure knowledge' (Pocock, p. 62).

This rhetorical approach was closely connected to the general development of Florentine **humanism**. Hulliung (p. 9) notes that 'Around 1400 … a "civic humanism" emerged when those intellectuals who studied ancient languages and art forms began to revive ancient political ideals in response to the life and death struggles of the Florentine republic.'

There was, more specifically relevant to Machiavelli's thought, a return to **classical sources** of political theory, notably to Aristotle's *Politics*. From these sources came a new interest in the complexity of real-world decision-making and institutions. The instability of their state, combined with the richness of their culture, led Florentine thinkers to propound a highly developed analysis of power politics.

Gaining and losing power

2

AIMS

* This chapter looks at Machiavelli's definition of modern politics. His 'Prince' is seen to be the archetype of a modern political leader.

* We see *The Prince* as expression of the pragmatic psychology of power.

READING *THE PRINCE* CHAPTERS 1-VI

The Prince 1-11: The new ruler

I *'Different kinds of States, and the different ways to get them'*

Machiavelli makes two key distinctions at the beginning of *The Prince*. The first is between republics and princely states: this division followed from the classical theories of Aristotle. Its lasting importance lies in the idea that we must start all political analysis by looking at the nature of the state. Hulliung reviewing the history of responses to Machiavelli as a whole concludes that 'the most vexing problem of Machiavelli interpretation' (p. 4) is the relation of monarchical and republican dimensions. In his other major work of political theory, *The Discourses*, Machiavelli takes a strongly republican line – how, critics have wondered, does this affect the emphasis on princely rule in this work? These relations are the subject of continuing debate, but there remains, across both texts, a consistent concern with power politics and the arts it requires – and with the psychology of leadership, which will form the focus of our reading. It is true, taking Machiavelli's thought as a whole, that the preference is for republican systems, but even there, his model is the powerful Roman empire, not a benign and modest independence.

For the purposes of *The Prince* then, Machiavelli focuses on the princely states, and makes a second distinction, between two kinds of ruler. One type of prince comes from an established ruling family. Their authority is stable, and so he is accepted as the legitimate successor – accepted by the people, the nobles and the institutions. The other kind of prince is 'new': he has no family authority behind his claim to power. He has to make his own position – to win acceptability from the people and nobles. He is, in Hannah Pitkin's terms, a 'Founder'.

This beginning indicates a key feature of Machiavelli's method of argument – the making of distinctions:

* *Types of state*: the book does have behind it a systematizing approach to political theory. Machiavelli is producing an overall scheme of types of ruler, state.

* At the centre of the theory of the state is the distinction between *two kinds of political authority*: long time or inherited, and new. This compares closely with the approach to political history taken in Holinshed's *Chronicles* of the English kings, source of Shakespeare's histories. For both Machiavelli and Shakespeare, political drama arises with the *new* ruler.

In the guided reading that follows, we will see how almost all modern leaders are illuminated by being compared with Machiavelli's new prince. It turns out that modern politics is richly illuminated by this account of the Renaissance princely state!

II *'On Hereditary Principates'*

Next, therefore, we see Machiavelli concisely dismissing from view all states that remain stable, where the prince is accepted simply because the ruling family has remained in control for as long as people can remember. For this thinker, there is nothing to reason interestingly about in these cases. Politics becomes a subject for reasoning only with the establishment of a *new* regime. This contrast between pre-rational tradition and the new world of reason must be seen in its wider philosophical context.

Here we can see an important way in which Machiavelli is a modern thinker.

MODERN MACHIAVELLI

Enlightenment:

The contrast between a rational world and one governed by tradition lies at the heart of 'modern enlightenment'. This contrast is present in thinkers as different as Marx and Mill and it remains central to contemporary philosophy. Machiavelli is in this sense an early thinker of the Enlightenment, one for whom politics begins where tradition ends. To say that the world is rational does not mean that everything comes out reasonably: on the contrary! Though in a more specific context, critics have rightly pointed to the gulf between the Renaissance and the later Enlightenment (see Skinner and Hulliung), there is in this general sense a close affinity between Machiavelli and later rational theorists.

The Prince III: Losing power

III 'On Mixed Principalities'

Machiavelli now zooms in on the theme that really grips his pragmatic imagination. Why does trouble arise in states? The first answer is that there is always likely to be trouble when a new state arises – that is, a state created by the claims of a new prince, rather than the continuation of inherited authority. We can summarize a rule:

Machiavellian Rule of Opportunity

A new state is never stable.

OR

The possibility of winning power always carries that of losing power.

This Machiavellian Rule of Opportunity generates, as we will see, many modern parallels.

There emerges from *The Prince* a gripping theory of *the paradoxes of success*: this will be seen to be one key to Machiavelli's political psychology.

Machiavellian Political Psychology

* *There is no such thing as pure success. Within the moment of achievement are the seeds of the reversal.*
* *The explanation is not fate or moral destiny, but the nature of human relationships and human reactions to specific circumstances: a pragmatic psychology.*

Machiavelli is particularly interested by one set of political circumstances, where the new state is 'mixed'.

KEY CONCEPT: 'MIXED [PRINCIPALITY]'

In a mixed state, power has been extended over an area that does not fit in. This added region is one that does not naturally belong to the new rulers. The people are different, perhaps they speak another language, follow a rival religion or recognize contrasting traditions.

This is a key reason for difficulties in maintaining power and one that tends to go with the arrival of the new prince. His new claims often include other territories – or he may be the representative of a rival state or authority.

Another Machiavellian Rule follows, one that applies to situations that arise when new forces enter a state from outside. Take an area. There are various conflicts – as a result, some groups are doing well at the expense of the others. In comes the new, ambitious power. Who sides with him? The Machiavellian Rule can be summarized as:

> ## Machiavellian Rule of Inversion
>
> ***The weakest groups are the natural allies of an invader – and hence the future ruling class of a new order.***

The exploited or oppressed are the ones who rush over to the intruder – and as a result they may be converted suddenly into the new top class!

Here Machiavelli draws attention to the determining influence of the least powerful group under certain circumstances. When an outside power intervenes, the weakest groups move towards it and they can then be transformed into the most powerful players in the game. We see a paradox by which weakness turns out to be strength, an analysis that foreshadows the nineteenth-century thinker Nietzsche's discussion of the power of the weak against the strong.

Machiavelli is interested in such general rules in so far as they come to life in the presence of specific examples. Each case is also distinct. His literary power balances his philosophical vision. So when he comes to the first big paradigm case, King Louis of France, who failed to hold new possessions in Italy, the analysis focuses on what seems unpredictable and surprising.

We meet King Louis in the midst of a crisis. He has taken control of one of the major Italian centres, Milan. What strategy will keep this new territory? He decides to be cunning and forms an alliance with the powerful Borgia pope, Alexander VI, father of Cesare whom we encounter shortly. The outcome is disastrous. Instead of increasing his own strength, Louis' strategy aids his rival, the Borgia, and effectively reduces his own power. Relentlessly, Machiavelli catalogues Louis' errors – the mistakes of a new prince trying to keep hold of a mixed principality. The key errors are:

* the *suppression of the weaker groups* in his new state – these could have been his natural allies

❋ the *inadvertent strengthening of a strong rival* through a temporary alliance.

Effectively, Louis has made the error that in modern times is known as 'appeasement' – he has pandered to the strong powers, both within and beyond Milan. As a result, he loses the territory – Lombardy – that he had gained.

Machiavelli insists that no accidental misfortune is needed to account for Louis' loss:

KEY QUOTE
None of this is in any way miraculous, but perfectly ordinary and reasonable.

(Norton edn, p.11)

Anatomy of key quote

○ '*miraculous*': this begins a scientific approach to politics or political science. The miraculous is that for which there is no generally viable explanation. Machiavelli's is interested in an alternative: reasons and general laws.

○ '*ordinary and reasonable*': Machiavelli examines the credibility of historical examples – by the light of everyday reason.

We have now seen how Machiavelli swiftly defines the topic of his great work through a combination of general concepts and specific cases. He asks what remains a fundamental question for news analysts and political historians, as well as for practical politicians: why do rulers so often take actions that rebound against their own interests? This is a genuinely *pragmatic* question, in the sense that it forces us to think more closely about specific circumstances, rather than allowing us to wander off into realms of grand speculation.

We can also see another key feature of Machiavelli's particular pragmatism, his negative and critical twist of mind. *The Prince* is the modern world's handbook of political fallacies, a great collection of 'how not tos'. For Machiavelli, rulers make their greatest mistakes not when their judgement is distorted by emotion or unreason, but through the weaknesses of false reasoning, and one of his main aims is to identify the most frequent of these errors. That is the basis of any positive advice which he is going to venture.

Looking at the failure of Louis, Machiavelli adds another pragmatic rule. Prefacing this observation, he effectively defines what he means by rules:

KEY CONCEPT: 'RULE'

For Machiavelli, a 'rule' is an observation which is:

* *generalizable*
* *applicable to* almost *all relevant cases.*

A Machiavellian Rule is based on observation and experience and it is tested by its ability to apply to related examples – with a small margin for rogue instances. Then we have a rule that applies to the failure to keep a hold on the state. Machiavelli is interested in explanations that centre on wrong choices, rather than on bad circumstances or unpredictable accidents. So from this discussion of political failure, we can readily formulate a Rule:

Machiavellian Rule of Non-appeasement

If you make someone else stronger, you make yourself weaker.

Here we see in action Machiavelli's notion of rational explanation, which centres on the twists and turns of human calculation. Louis thinks he is being cunning by strengthening his allies in Italy. In fact, he is preparing the way for his own failure. Such reasoning is the key to why rulers act against their own interests and the basis of this book of political fallacies. It is not that Louis' judgement is distorted by emotion or unreason; rather, he epitomizes the weaknesses of false reasoning. This is a fundamentally 'enlightenment' analysis.

MODERN MACHIAVELLI

* *Machiavelli's approach has affinities with the Marxist theory of false consciousness or ideology – acting on the basis of the wrong sense of own interests and particularly of who is on which side.*

* *His theory also has deep affinities with* contemporary political psychology, *as in the work of Jon Elster. Like Machiavellian pragmatic psychology, this new political theory is about how people misunderstand their specific situation, not about political irrationality, but about the mistaken use of reason.*

The Prince IV–VI: How to hold on

Machiavelli's fourth chapter begins with a political conundrum drawn from classical history. Why, he asks, did Alexander the Great succeed in founding a stable regime in territories that he took over – such as the huge empire of the Persians that he won from Darius? How did Alexander succeed when, as Machiavelli has just shown, so many others have failed? Why, in particular, did his heirs stay in power over an alien region? On the way to his explanation, Machiavelli makes a contrast between two kinds of state structure. In the first, the 'Turkish', the state is centralized and all local authority derives only from that centre. In the second, the 'French', there are dispersed and rival centres of power. The 'Turkish' kind of state is hard to win, because it has such a strong core, but once taken, it is easy to keep, as long as you can preserve the dominance of the centre. Conversely, you may win a French-style state more easily, since you can play off the rival factions and regions against one another. But then you will also fall victim in turn to the same fissures and conflicts.

IV *'Why the Successors of Alexander after his death did not lose the kingdom he had conquered from Darius'*

Here we encounter the game-playing aspect of Machiavelli's thought. This aspect of Machiavelli has strong affinities with an important field of modern social and economic science, called game theory. This analogy has been noted by recent commentators, for example Hanna Pitkin in her analysis of Machiavelli as a distinctively *political* thinker. In modern terms, Machiavelli regards politics as if it were a zero sum game, where every gain implies a corresponding loss. Machiavelli's pragmatic rule of the political game-playing can be stated:

Machiavellian Rule of Zero Sum Power

If power is easier to win, it is harder to keep.

The degree of political difficulty is constant, or, you can say, politics never gets any easier. For Machiavelli the pragmatist, with his interest in how to handle circumstances, it is a mistake to assume that some situations are easier to handle than others. The difficulty changes, it does not disappear. Or you could say that there is a principle of instability. If the state is unstable before you take over, then it will be unstable afterwards too.

V *'How Cities or States should be ruled, which lived by their own laws before being taken'*

Game-playing is a way of thinking about strategy and *The Prince* aims to identify the possible strategies for holding onto new power, new possessions. So, he says, Alexander had only to preserve the institutions of the state he acquired. It was centralized: he just needed to take over the centre and the rest followed.

Machiavelli moves on to reflect on the wider problems of strategy. Here we encounter the ruthless side of *The Prince*, as Machiavelli considers more broadly how to hang on to cities that you have deprived of their independence. There are three options:

* total obliteration

* moving in yourself

* creating a sympathetic government that you can manipulate and using it to raise resources.

Now *The Prince* emerges as an art of 'policy'. The key feature of the book as a work on policy-making is this sense of **rationally analysable alternatives**. Machiavellian policy is the art of recognizing the options and judging their different possible outcomes.

It often seems, in modern-day coverage, as if 'policy issues' are dull. Whenever politicians demand that we debate policies, rather than getting distracted by personalities, they are really acknowledging their failure to make policy humanly interesting. Machiavelli, by contrast, brings policy vividly to life, as a field of risk and calculation, one which requires imagination at full stretch. Policy is *the* field for the Machiavellian pragmatic imagination. In here lie the roots of what Hulliung calls the 'scandal' of Machiavelli's thought – and the difficulty of reconciling his ideas easily with the more comforting forms of humanism.

In the case above, keeping control over a newly acquired city, the list of options seems brutal. But one could say that Machiavelli is simply confronting us with the possibilities. From America in South Vietnam to the Soviet Union in Afghanistan, big powers have often shared Machiavelli's map of possibilities: destroy; move in; set up a puppet state.

The chilling option, of course, is obliteration. Machiavelli does not let us wriggle off this hook. He stresses that the only sure-fire option is annihilation. This is really a way of exposing **the paradoxes of political rationality**: the self-defeating side of rational decision-making. After all, what have you actually won by this strategy? We will be considering some modern cases, such as the United States in Vietnam and Russia in Chechnya. The terrible Machiavellian irony reappears in history: if you have an absolute will to keep hold of a territory, the logic of your aim drives you to destroy what you wish to keep. This can be seen as the cynicism of Machiavelli. But it can equally well be seen as his alternative to tragedy – the roots of disaster are found in the nature of calculation and circumstances.

Machiavelli concludes this bleak review by reflecting that republics are even more dangerous to acquire than another ruler's kingdom. For republics – having a loyalty to the state among the populace – will never give in. They will fight harder and they are always liable to start fighting afresh when you think you have won. Consider the modern Yugoslavian case, where rival republics were unleashed against one another in the aftermath of the break-up of a synthetic union or mixed principality under communist hereditary rule. Machiavelli anticipates the link between violence and the traditions of autonomy. This analysis prepares the way for the theory of modern nationalism – states with which the population fiercely identifies.

> VI *'About New Princedoms Acquired with one's own arms and energy (virtu)'*

Machiavelli now introduces the central concept of 'virtu', just as we are reaching the darkest and perhaps most cynical aspects of his opening argument.

KEY CONCEPT: 'VIRTU'

'Virtue' usually refers to a moral quality. But in this context, 'virtu' means something closer to positive action and will, rather than the modern-day moral sense.

This idea has been a focal point in the interpretation of Machiavelli. The nineteenth-century authority, Burkhardt, gave the most influential definition, seeing this virtu as 'a union of force and ability ... force of ability'. Hannah Pitkin, the contemporary feminist scholar, illuminates this fundamental conception of 'virtu' by seeing it in terms of a notion of 'manhood' centring on 'autonomy'. Using his concept of 'virtu', above all, Machiavelli defines what can be stated as a pragmatic rule:

Machiavellian Rule of Virtu (Risk)

The more you leave things to sort themselves out, the weaker your hold on power.

OR

If you want to be safe, you must take the risk of acting on your own judgement.

What interests Machiavelli is the lack of 'virtu': the less you make your own choice, the more you will be a victim of other forces. As Pitkin (p. 156) puts it: 'Where men are lazy or apathetic, lacking in virtu, fortune controls all by default.' This rule of risk shows Machiavelli as a theorist of political reason. His approach to reason is quite unfamiliar by modern standards. We tend to see reason in contrast to the irrational, two aspects of the human psyche. But in *The Prince* reason is not defined as against irrational emotion, but against trusting to fortune. This is one of the key points of the book: the polarity is not rational/emotional but rational/leaving to chance.

Our Rule of Risk is also the start of Machiavelli's complex reflections on trust. He gives great importance to misplaced trust in many different forms: misplaced trust of people, of the future, of luck itself. There is an inverse relationship between trust and risk-taking. Machiavellian Reason replaces trust in chance by conscious risk-taking. Again, you could see a cynical potential within the pragmatism: never take a situation on trust, at face value.

Machiavelli then moves from this pragmatic Rule of Risk to the drama of individual leaders and would-be rulers. He distinguishes the case of the 'lucky' ones, who are handed power, and the others, who have won power. These latter have succeeded through force of personality, Machiavellian virtu. As ever, Machiavelli applies a zero sum logic: if you came to power easily, you will have difficulty keeping control. Political difficulty is, as it were, conserved.

It is also characteristic that Machiavelli's imagination is fired by the more difficult situation, that of those who have struggled for power – just as he gravitates intellectually to the new state as against the hereditary one. His is the logic of the zero sum game: the harder the winning, the more chance of hanging on. This is the core of Machiavelli's theory of political 'virtu'. He then moves on to a still more difficult situation, that of the prince who has to recreate the entire state in order to assume power. He acknowledges that this is the most challenging of all tasks. Nothing is riskier than the creation of 'a new order', with new institutions, new forms of legitimacy.

The greatest risk is the one that appeals to Machiavelli – because it allows the fullest expression of virtu, of active will and positive calculation. Here is his political free market, the sphere of the political risk-takers. Machiavelli's heroes are those who have come closest to making their own circumstances. His pragmatism is not about caution or the middle ground. On the contrary: it is about controlling one's situation in the fullest possible measure. We will see the applications of this theory of the new prince and the new order throughout our discussion – notably in the world after the Cold War and also after the European empires.

Machiavelli even approaches the concept of the modern revolutionary. He looks at those visionaries who have seized power. What you find, he argues, is that it is not the vision itself that makes the crucial difference. The kind of visionary who succeeds is the one who is also 'armed'. There is a strong link from this idea both to religious wars and to political revolution. Machiavelli's militant prophet foreshadows the theory of the revolutionary vanguard. Machiavelli is the reverse of a conventional pragmatist in some ways: to adapt to your situation, to respond to circumstances, that may often require the most daring and extreme action. Nothing is riskier than survival.

THE PRINCE CHAPTERS 1–VI ILLUSTRATIONS: MACHIAVELLI AND THE THIRD MILLENNIUM

We have now traced the logic of Machiavelli's opening arguments, across a series of distinctions: republic/princely; hereditary/new; single/mixed state; difficult to win/easy to win; coming to power through effort/being given power. But there is also an immense imaginative power to Machiavelli's ideas and this is now our theme.

The real importance of *The Prince* lies less in the subtlety of its reasoned distinctions, great though these are, than in the way its ideas stick to the world. This quality defines what we have called Machiavelli's **pragmatic imagination** – rooted in his pragmatic psychology of political power and struggle. His ideas have a unique ability to get inside specific situations, however far removed from his own.

A Machiavellian moment

We look now, as an example, at the way Machiavelli's first six chapters can be applied to the political order of the third millennium, which, it will be suggested, can be understood as 'a Machiavellian moment'. In 1991 the Soviet Union was dissolved. In place of a unitary, though strained, state there arose myriad struggling and fragmented new states, the post-USSR states such as the giant Russian Federation, Georgia and Armenia. These are 'new' states with new princes in a precisely Machiavellian sense. The Communist Party had ruled the USSR for 70 years, and it had given legitimacy to a series of ruling princes. Each prince was rooted in the authority of that hereditary family. But take away that party or family – and suddenly the new princes are on their own, with their new states. Let us consider some of the variations on this theme. (The accounts that follow draw on recent media analysis and specifically on the specialist journal *Transitions* and its website *Transitions On Line*.)

The new prince problem

Take the case of Georgia. Here is one of the largest of these new states facing the new millennium. Georgia is a huge region, birthplace of the most notorious Soviet dictator, Stalin. It faces the new century locked into a struggle with Russia, its even larger neighbour. The Georgian new state had tried to turn to Western Europe, but was blocked by Russia, its more powerful rival. In addition, within Georgia, there was a maze of local conflicts, rooted in demands for regional autonomy.

This situation makes crystalline sense in terms of our Machiavellian pragmatic rule:

Machiavellian Rule of Opportunity

A new state is never stable.

OR

The possibility of winning power implies that of losing it.

Though nominally a republic, Georgia is clearly cast in a princely mode, with its new prince, Eduard Shevardnadze, favoured by the West where he had been familiar as the last foreign minister of the Soviet regime. Here, then, we have the new prince and the full extremity of the position – new as against hereditary, and also needing to introduce a new political order to stand any chance of survival. Shevardnadze is an example of what Pitkin (p. 52) calls the Machiavellian figure of 'the Founder', the man who stands at the origin of the new state.

Then another of Machiavelli's concepts comes into play – the 'mixed' principality, which is often a side effect or association of the rise of a new prince:

Unable to fulfil even basic functions of the state, the Georgian government had little opportunity in 1999 to consolidate its power in the country's diverse regions. Relations with the breakaway republics of Abkhazia and South Ossetia did not improve … Tbilisi also clashed repeatedly with the autonomous republic of Ajara, nominally the home of Muslim Georgians … In Abkhazia proper, physical hostilities were at a minimum in 1999, but both sides continued to wage a bitter propagandas war … In May, the South Ossetians held illegal elections … Ajara's leader Aslan Abashidze considers the Shevardnadze government to be only minimally legitimate.

All this fits the theory of the 'Mixed Principality' which is where the troubles of the new prince are multiplied by the acquisition of alien territories. In this case, the new states are being recreated by developments inside the existing state of Georgia, which is itself new in another way. In other words, Georgia is being remade as a mixed principality from within rather than by conquest or diplomacy. These manifold uprisings all meet the Machiavellian criterion: difference of language and of tradition.

Rebellions arise and again we can grasp their significance in Machiavellian terms. They are led by the ringleaders of the old order. Here is the other side of the Machiavellian Rule that the weakest turn to the new power – those who did well under the old order can never be trusted. There is no way to win over these loyalists – they will always try to recreate the lost state.

Machiavellian violence
Take a second type of case in the post-USSR world. Armenia is another new state and increasingly remade as a mixed principality

from within. The Communist Party has been in power for seven decades, based on its Moscow centre. Effectively, Armenia too has belonged to the Soviet hereditary principate of one-party rule. Authority has held because people have got so used to obeying it. Now the new state is riven by rivalries. There is a specific Machiavellian dimension to the Armenian example. At the centre of the Armenian crisis, there is an episode of extreme political violence, with the shadow of court conspiracy:

> *The year of 1999 ended on a bitter and shocking note: the 27 October assassination of Prime Minister Vazgen Sarkisian, Parliamentary Speaker Karen Demirchian, and several other government officials.*

Here is a crisis of a new state, yielding atrocity. There is a chain of events involving three princes or would-be princes: Sarkisian, the final Victim, Kocharian, a Rival, and the Old Leader or prince, Ter Petrossian. The Victim and Rival have been involved in a struggle, after co-operating to remove the Old Prince. In fact, the eventual Victim had been brought in by the Old Prince, as a last throw of the dice, which fits our fundamental Machiavellian Rule:

Machiavellian Rule of Non-appeasement

If you make someone else stronger, you make yourself weaker.

This Rule applies twice: first to the Old Prince and then to the one who becomes the Victim of the coup. Each makes alliances that lead towards his downfall, violently in the second case: 'In the aftermath of the shootings, recriminations and accusations multiplied.'

It seems that all three would-be new princes failed to abide by our Machiavellian Rule: never form an alliance that might strengthen your enemies. The Old Prince brought in the man who then removed him, but that act involved a second alliance that in turn produced a coup.

Keeping the city

Finally, we can briefly consider Russia and Chechnya, the darkest side of the Machiavellian millennium. Here we have the break-up of the Russian Federation – of which the most spectacular aspect is the Chechen war. Chechnya is a break-away republic within the Russian Federation. In response to the break-away movement, the Russian army invades – twice – and the second time levels the capital Grozny. In this story, the dramatis personae are: the Russian leaders, Boris Yeltsin and then Vladimir Putin; and the Chechen leader, Mashkhadov. In Machiavellian terms, Chechnya is an alien region – being reborn within the Russian state, which then tries to reconquer it.

Following our pragmatic Machiavellian Rule, we see that these unstable structures invite bids for power and also bring about their failure. It is now easier for people like Mashkhadov, and even Putin at the centre, to rise to power – but, by the same token, they have to spend far more energy holding on than under the old system.

Machiavellian Rule of Zero Sum Politics

If power is easier to win, it is harder to keep.

The response, to the whole anarchic mix, the terrible Russian invasion, can also be analysed in Machiavellian terms:

Military command issued a warning in early December to the residents of Grozny announcing that civilians had until 10 December to leave the city or be subjected to a military offensive.

Here we can apply Machiavelli's paradox of political rationality – that the only absolute way to retain control is to destroy the city. He illustrates it by referring to the Romans' destruction of Carthage; we have the contemporary case of Grozny.

3 Luck and judgement

AIMS

This chapter is about Machiavelli's treatment of political luck. What is the relationship between luck and judgement in political success?

* Our chapter has as its first, and most sustained, focus Machiavelli's intellectual encounter with the career of Cesare Borgia and with the theme of political cruelty. We see how Borgia represents the prince who rises by luck but seeks to continue by judgement.

* The theme is then continued with two contrasting cases. First there is Agathocles, a classical Greek villain, who embodies, for Machiavelli, the truly evil career, which is also the example of pure judgement, with almost no luck.

* In contrast to both Agathocles and Borgia, there is the prince who comes to power through popular choice, the most republican of the princes and the precursor of many democratic rulers.

READING *THE PRINCE* CHAPTERS VII–VIII: THE MACHIAVELLIAN VILLAIN

The Prince VII: The risk of politics

> VII 'About New States acquired with other people's arms and by Good Luck'

Now Machiavelli is looking at the different types of personality to be found among new princes. First, and least impressive, are the ones who come to power by favour of fortune and the efforts of others. They arrive easily, but afterwards comes the struggle, and few lucky ones have the type of character to flourish in such an aftermath.

The argument then closes in on the fall of the lucky ones, which is the subject of so many tragedies. Machiavelli's is not a theory of the tragic flaw, but of the one mistake. Like political commentators who are his heirs, Machiavelli is transfixed by that one moment of error which is sufficient to overturn a lifetime of good luck and right judgements. There is no luck so great that a moment's bad judgement cannot waste it; there is no judgement so fine that a moment's bad luck cannot thwart it. The balance is always in favour of misfortune.

Machiavelli has reached Cesare Borgia, the paradigm case. His notorious career comes in three phases, according to *The Prince*:

* First there is **the rise**, which is due to luck. Borgia is brought to power by the luck of being Pope Alexander's son.

* Then there is a second phase, **the time of judgement**, when Borgia succeeds in capitalizing on this initial good fortune.

* But then there comes a third phase, **the reversal**, fall and death.

Borgia's life is a three act drama. But it is not a tragedy, for Machiavelli. His interest is in the idea that Borgia is the one who almost succeeded, as compared to the run-of-the mill case, like King Louis who made every mistake imaginable.

At the centre, there is Machiavelli's pragmatic emphasis on the single mistake – the disastrous miscalculation rather than the tragic flaw. Machiavelli is a prolific theorist, but among his many overlapping Rules, Ironies and Paradoxes, this theory of the flaw is probably at the centre. Here we can formulate:

The Machiavellian Rule of Error

One error is worth a thousand right decisions and a million lucky breaks.

This is a pragmatic theory in the sense that it is created through synthesizing specific cases and also because it deals with the world of specific and localized circumstances. The process is different in every case. Machiavelli is not saying the fall is inevitable; he is no tragic thinker. On the contrary, there was always a chance of success – it is just not very likely in the long run. This pragmatic theory of error is one of Machiavelli's main contributions to the theory of decision-making.

Let us follow Machiavelli's history of Cesare Borgia, the nearly-man of *The Prince*. In the first phase, Cesare is the recipient of his father's gifts. Alexander, the Borgia pope, is seen pursuing a deliberate strategy designed to bring power to his son. Specifically, he creates trouble among existing states in order to exploit the resulting turmoil.

Machiavellian Rule of Strategic Opportunism

Don't wait for opportunities: make your own trouble and then exploit it.

Cesare becomes ruler of the Romagna, through these efforts.

But the favoured son is important to Machiavelli because he understood that he could not keep by luck what he gained by it. In the second phase, he becomes the active agent of his own fate and thus an instance of Machiavellian virtu.

KEY QUOTE
Hence the duke decided he would no longer depend on the weapons and fortune of others.

(Norton edn, p.20)

In this middle phase, Borgia has entered the sphere of what modern social science would call rational choice. He makes a decision not to trust either fortune or the goodwill of others. This narrative is at the heart of both Machiavelli's arguments and his later reputation. The story includes legendary cruelties and treacheries. In particular, we see Cesare's ruthless elimination of his potential rivals. First he seems to favour at least the supporters of the Orsini and Colona clans, his main rivals in the political world of Rome. He lies, he is almost paranoiacally treacherous. After a time of apparent beneficence he takes the moment and kills off the entire Orsini clan. He also takes care to cultivate the most frightening possible image. Then, bolstered by this reputation and the terror it inspires, he casts aside all his earlier allies, particularly the French on whom he had relied at a previous stage.

As Hannah Pitkin argues, Machiavelli seems to place the highest value on this pursuit of 'autonomy'. The manipulation of others is all in pursuit of this strategy of absolute independence. Ultimately, this goes back to Rules we have formulated earlier, especially the:

Machiavellian Rule of Virtu (Risk)

The more you leave things to sort themselves out, the weaker your hold on power.

OR

If you want to be safe, you must take the risk of acting on your own judgement.

The detail is medieval. But the themes are shared with modern rational choice theory: trust and reputation. Like his modern counterparts, Machiavelli sees the use of reputation in reducing the need to trust to others.

But then there is the notorious cruelty. Borgia employs a brutal minister to subdue a new acquisition. When the unpopularity starts to rebound, Borgia knows what to do: he waits to make sure the people blame the minister, Remirro del Orro, and not himself, the true source. The populace wake one morning and find the dreaded minister in the town square – cut in two. Here we have the crux of Machiavellian violence. The issue is the *uses* of violence, not just violence for its own sake, or as a 'natural' fact.

But in many ways, the most important phase of Cesare's career is still to come: **the fall**. At first it seems the theme is bad luck. He tries to win the support of Spain – and he is succeeding. He will be able to use this support to replace his original dependence on the French. Then his father, Alexander VI, dies. The Spanish lose interest, once Cesare has lost his base. Borgia is all set and then his father the pope dies just before he has sealed his new alliances. In addition, he is doubly unlucky, becoming ill himself. Machiavelli draws on his own personal experience as the Florentine envoy to Borgia. Cesare is said to have told Niccolo personally that he had everything worked out – he had taken into account what might be happening when his father died. But he had not expected his own illness.

Even when all is going wrong, Cesare has such a fierce reputation that nobody moves against him. Then Machiavelli slips in a different perspective. It seems Borgia also made a *mistake*. In response to his father's death, he supported one of the candidates for pope, a man who had in fact been an old enemy – Julius. For Machiavelli this was his single mistake, in a career of countless decisions and risks. It was a wrong decision – and not just any wrong decision. Previously, Cesare had offended this man. Now he tries to cultivate him. But the favour will not be repaid! Cesare has failed to recognize one of the central Machiavellian rules – not building up the strength of a potential enemy. To the extent that Julius becomes stronger, Cesare's own position must get weaker – in line with our Machiavellian Rule of Non-appeasement.

This is the direct turning-point. Once you make a mistake, then you have left a gap through which bad luck can flood. That is why one error is worth countless right judgements, the central Rule of Error. Machiavelli sees the fatal error in terms of his pragmatic psychology. That is, he looks at the situation in terms of the make-up of the character and the motives. He also looks at how that character is reacting to particular circumstances. For Machiavellian pragmatic psychology, the outcome is always uncertain. This theory enables you to focus on how a person reacts to a changing situation and so brings about his or her own demise, in this unique case.

The Prince VIII: The political villains

VIII *'On those who have become princes by crime'*

Machiavelli's account of Borgia certainly does not draw a moral, though he does present pragmatic conclusions. He is aware, though, that others will find the absence of morality disturbing. In the next section, Machiavelli gives a wider account of the whole sphere of political villainy. Now the moral judgements appear unequivocal; we are dealing with criminals, those who resort to evil deeds. However, there is a twist. These figures emerge, in Machiavelli's theory, as a type of modern man. These villains are precursor figures of modernity – the risk-takers as against the fatalists. They are the ones who refuse to accept their given condition and who seek to make their own luck.

The paradigm case is Agathocles, who rises through the ranks of the Greek army to seize power. Agathocles had risen to become a member of the officer corps – classic coup material! He sets up a conspiracy against the established ruling class. The troops are ready – a signal is given and a state occasion turns into a massacre. Down go the senators and with them the wealthy merchants. It is a populist army coup.

Machiavelli does not discard the moral conventions. But he also draws a pragmatic conclusion. He makes two equally significant points about this Agathocles:

* He is an evil man.

* He lives in a way that leaves nothing to chance.

Is this, then, the Machiavellian poison – evil is alright, if it works?

Here we are focusing more closely on some of the origins of Machiavelli's notoriety. His treatment of Agathocles leads into a series of reflections on the uses of violence to attain political goals:

KEY QUOTE

Cruelty can be described as well used ... when it is performed all at once, for reason of self-preservation ... badly used, when it is infrequent at first, but increases with time instead of diminishing.

(Norton edn, p.27)

Anatomy of key quote

o *'Cruelty'*: this is a founding issue in modern politics and ideology. Leading modern theorists from Freud to Foucault and Rorty have seen cruelty as the key to understanding power.

o *'used'*: this argument is not a defence of cruelty as such. It is an analysis of political calculation.

o *'for reason of'*: we can consider such arguments in relation to the 'means and ends' debate that still defines much discussion of politics and ethics. When do the ends justify the means? Machiavelli sees the argument for self-preservation as the strongest version of an end justifying means.

o *'performed all at once'*: Machiavelli's ideas can also be explored in a modern context with reference to revolutionary and terrorist violence. When is the violent incident justified? This Machiavellian theme was pursued by the modern thinker, Hannah Arendt.

o *'badly used'*: as we will see, this produces a rich way of explaining or expounding the collapse of dictatorial regimes.

The way is now open to the debate about Machiavellianism – which is really a debate about modernity itself. Can there be an all-encompassing set of ethical values in the modern world? Or are some spheres of decision-making independent of ethics? Is modern society a world where morality becomes one among other discourses, along with science, policy, psychology and art? Or does moral judgement still have the pride of place? Machiavelli posed these fundamental problems that have perplexed social and political theorists of the modern order. His ambiguity is well expressed by Hannah Pitkin's (p. 3) observation that 'Niccolo Machiavelli may well be the most political of all the great political theorists; and, like politics itself, Machiavelli horrifies and repels us, yet also attracts and fascinates.'

Machiavelli elaborates his argument and we can see in it the seeds of a distinction between revolution and totalitarian state. He moves into direct advice – quite sparingly used. If you come to power, in a new state, you must take stock. Look at your enemies or possible rivals. Total up all the harm you need to inflict – and get it all out of the way in one great initial instant of barbarity.

By contrast, if you leave things to brew, hostile forces will go on growing. Then you will find your regime on the slide. As your hold on power slips, you find yourself resorting to increasingly desperate measures of repression.

Machiavellian Rule of Crisis

Emergency measures are, by definition, too late.

Here is a key ingredient in Machiavelli's pragmatic psychology of political misfortune. A particular synergy links bad judgement and ill luck. Certain motives lead to misjudgement and that then opens the floodgates of bad luck, which in turn makes new misjudgement more likely. This is *how* the powerful become unlucky – they make their own bad luck, by not acting in advance.

THE PRINCE CHAPTERS VII–VIII APPLICATIONS: THE NEW MACHIAVELLIAN VILLAINY

Historical methodology

We have now seen how Machiavelli advances extremely subtly across the dangerous terrain of political villainy. His arguments are rich in reasons, which does not stop them being lastingly controversial. They also have, however, that other Machiavellian power: the imaginative force of sticking to new and changing situations.

Now we take this Machiavellian approach to the current case of Slobodan Milosovic in Serbia. In presenting such an example, we follow a long tradition that has interpreted Machiavelli via current figures and vice versa. For example, the seventeenth-century English historian Clarendon explored Machiavelli's account of Borgia in terms of Oliver Cromwell (see F. Raab, *The English Face of Machiavelli*, pp. 150–4):

> *Whereas, on the other side, Cromwell, and the few others with whom he consulted, first considered what was absolutely necessary to their main and determined end, and then, whether it were right or wrong, to make all other means subservient to it; to cozen and deceive men, as long as they could induce them to contribute to what they desired.*

Clarendon employs a version of what we can here term 'Machiavellian methodology' – he is not approving of Cromwell's approach, but he is trying to understand the thinking at work, how it arises in the world and its relation to elements of what might be called ordinary political conduct.

Clarendon is trying to define and test Machiavellian rules, just as we now do:

> *Yet without doubt the rule will still hold good; and they who enter upon unwarrantable enterprises must pursue many unwarrantable ways to preserve themselves from the penalty of the first guilt.*

Clarendon in fact, as we noted above, refers to Machiavelli's 'method in speaking' (Raab, p. 151) as widely misunderstood or neglected by critics who leap to attack individual pronouncements. It provides this early modern historian with a basis for a critical analysis of the behaviour of a man he regarded as a tyrant in his own time – let us see how it fares now.

Milosovic: the rise to power

Slobodan Milosovic came to power in Yugoslavia at the end of the communist period. He retained control after the fall of communism. Here is a man who became a new prince surrounded by new states – the fragmenting world of the modern Balkans. He is for many *the* modern embodiment of political villainy – and has ended his career, at the time of writing, charged with war crimes in the Hague international court. To take a Machiavellian approach we need first to adopt a definition in which the post-Yugoslavian Balkans are seen as princely states, rather than their nominal form of republics. This seems fair – the politics of the region comes into focus around the power struggles of the new princes.

How far does a Machiavellian approach illuminate the rise and fall of Slobodan Milosovic? (In the account that follows our main source will be the specialist journal *Transitions* and its associated website.)

First, in line with the analysis of Borgia, there is the rise to power. In the late 1980s, various parties and institutes helped Milosovic to take over the Yugoslav state – and at that time also the ruling Communist Party. For example, he draws upon support from the Serbian Academy, a body of writers and academics. He rewards their acclaim diligently and attaches them to his own party as tightly as possible. Soon, many academicians are 'sitting on Milosovic's advisory councils'. But it does not last long! Together with other kingmakers, the Serbian academicians are cast aside. The break is brutal and takes the favoured ones aback:

Academy members' alienation from Milosevic widened in 1993, when Dobrina Cosic – a writer, academy member … was unceremoniously sacked.

Rely as briefly as possible on outside support and then discard: that is Milosovic's treatment of the Serbian Academy and Writer's Union. You can see the same pattern even more clearly in Milosovic's approach to the church. At the early stage, he draws them into his councils and makes many rich offers:

The church's relationship with Milosevic was purely a marriage of convenience … Milosevic promised nearly everything to the church.

Both sides think they are being cunning. But Milosovic is the first to break the deal: 'But those were empty promises.' Again after attaching the powerful actors to his own group, he makes certain he does not prolong the initial dependence. The writers, academicians and clergy join protests in November 1996 – but they are too late, like Borgia's initial allies.

Here we can directly apply Machiavellian Rules and in some detail reconstruct the thinking behind Milosovic's actions. Milosovic's early approach can be seen to correspond closely with several of the **pragmatic rules** of calculation promoted in *The Prince*. The most general approach is **not to become dependent on others**, our Rule of Virtu or Risk-Taking. Where a previous dependence has been necessary, break it as soon as possible. Milosovic shares this rule with Machiavelli's Borgia, who determined as he rose in power to break his reliance on the support of other people and groups. Milosovic also follows Machiavelli's account of Borgia's initial tactic. The Serbian began by drawing members of rival factions into his own party, just as Borgia did with the Orsini and the Colona clans in Machiavellian Rome. Borgia gave out pensions and status, just like his modern counterpart. Just so, the academicians and the intellectuals are taken on board. Then they are set adrift, as the Orsini were – realizing belatedly that they were on the road to ruin instead of fortune.

Milosovic: the middle phase

As the regime continues, you can see Milosovic still following the Borgia pattern. There are new arrests and censorship and draconian fines. This comes at a moment of relative calm on the international scene, after a time of brutal wars and atrocities. According to close observers:

> *Whenever Milosovic succeeds in finding a common language with the international community ... he has always used the space to strengthen his position within the country by getting rid of his political opponents.*

This fits the Borgia tactic, as defined by Machiavelli: **never allow rivals and potential opponents into the frame** – the application of a Machiavellian Rule of Non-appeasement. He also takes the Machiavellian approach to cruelty – do the harm early and comprehensively. This Machiavellian approach does not pre-empt our rights to judge – but it does enable us to speculate precisely, and using the facts, about the calculations made by political leaders in their particular circumstances, and to see general patterns at work.

Now we come to the core themes of cruelty and evil. Darkest of all, there is Milosovic's use of war and violence across the Balkans, in Bosnia and then in Kosovo. It seems likely that he has not merely responded to trouble in those places, but has actively fomented the disturbances. We can use Machiavelli to reconstruct a plausible state of mind and set of intentions – which is not an alternative to judgement, but a way of making such actions conceivable. What led a 'rational' man to act like that?

Here is 'a politician who has built his career by fuelling conflict over Kosovo'. The greater the scale of the uproar, the better it may serve his purposes. In this respect, too, Milosevic fits the Borgia pattern and indeed the context has affinities with Cesare's world of early Renaissance Italy, with fragmenting and rival states struggling and larger blocs intervening in their conflicts for their own purposes. This time the parallel is with the first phase of Cesare's career, where the active agent is his father, Pope Alexander, who, according to Machiavelli, created all the troubles that he could among surrounding states in order to make possible the rise to power of his family. It is Kosovo that shows Milosovic at his most similar to the Machiavellian Borgia family – father and son – in outlook. In the late 1980s, at the start, he goes down to the province to stir up trouble:

Kosovo Polje (Field of the Blackbirds), where the Serbs lost their fateful battle to the Ottomans in 1389 and where, 600 years later, Milosovic had his first open war cry before a cheering crowd of up to a million Serbs.

Minutes later, now addressing the crowd from a building, he exclaimed that there was "no need for the police to keep order. You do it yourself!"

Here he openly enacts the pragmatic rule followed by Borgia: create your own trouble, if none is forthcoming (our Rule of Strategic Opportunism).

Such actions also correspond to Machiavelli's associated picture of the ruthless Agathocles, who left nothing to chance and preferred calculated violence to passivity. Milosovic is a Machiavellian actor in the specific sense that he is a man who sets out to make his own luck. So in the unfolding story:

> *He went on to overthrow the confused leaders of Serbia, Montenegro, and Vojvodina, thus destroying the delicate balance of power in Yugoslavia.*

This, too, follows the rule of making your own trouble and also the more basic tactic of removing opponents followed by both father and son in the Renaissance case.

At this point, we can see the full power of *Machiavelli's pragmatic psychology*. His analyses, and their associated narratives, continue to stick to the world. He does not offer deep-level explanations. But his ideas draw together scattered circumstances. Through Machiavelli we can find patterns in the chaos of events. In the case of Milosovic, what Machiavelli offers can be called a method of 'detached empathy'. That is, Machiavelli's insights enable us to reconstruct a state of mind, a coherent intention and a game plan, within the opaque figure of the Serbian prince. We tend to think of empathy as involving sympathy. Machiavellian empathy is not sympathetic. It is not judgemental, perhaps, either. But there is a peculiar objective empathy within the ideas of *The Prince*.

Milosovic: the fall
What about the fall of Milosovic? Here we draw upon the central Machiavellian Rule of Error – the one mistake that is worth all the right judgements and moments of good luck. This Rule of Error applies to the endgames of both Milosevic and the Borgias. Eventually Milosevic runs aground. He sets off another war in Kosovo. But this provokes a North Atlantic Treaty Organization (NATO) bombing campaign against Serbia. Initially he seems to survive; in fact, his end has come. His regime is defeated in an

election that for once he fails to control. Soon he is facing war crimes
charges and is under arrest. We will see how this can be illuminated
by Machiavelli's method of searching for the fatal error.

But to take a Machiavellian approach means keeping a close eye on
the detail, looking carefully at how the rules of pragmatic psychology
apply. First, there is the fact that it is Kosovo which brings the
endgame. This is the original source of Milosevic's power and in
some ways the place where he formed certain lasting dependences.
From a Machiavellian perspective, the problem is that at last
Milosovic has failed to achieve complete autonomy and break
entirely his initial dependence on the support and resources of other
people. Here he still is dependent – which plays a key role in his **fatal
error**. He is drawn tighter into the Kosovo struggle, between his own
allies and the ethnic Albanian majority. This leads into the
miscalculation:

*There is also speculation as to the extent to which the
Serbian delegation was bargaining in good faith. Some
diplomats and analysts believe that Milosovic had already
calculated that he could accept 'a little bit of bombing' and
eventually work out a more satisfactory agreement.*

He decides to risk provoking the great powers. Maybe the bombing
by NATO will unify Serbia again. But he underestimates the scale of
the trouble:

*NATO began its bombing campaign of the Federal Republic
of Yugoslavia on 24 March ... both NATO and Milosovic
appear to have made many miscalculations about each
other's intentions prior to 24 March ... [the bombing
lasted] 78 days.*

From there, his power unravels. He is no longer able to suppress the
other side. In Machiavellian terms, Milosovic has committed his
fatal error. In other words, Machiavellian methodology leads you to

apply the central Rule of Error: look for the mistake that lies behind the moment of failure, after all that 'success'.

Now we close in on the endgame, prime material for a Machiavellian analysis. The end does not come immediately:

> *Despite all of these setbacks, however, at year's end Milosovic's grip on power in Belgrade was as strong as ever.*

This, too, belongs within the Machiavellian compass. Like Borgia, Milosovic has such a frightening reputation that the other side do not feel able to move immediately. Even as his power collapses, there is the fear he has consistently generated to fall back on. But all the time, Milosovic is off balance. There is another Machiavellian angle as the count of losses mounts.

> *During the eleven-week conflict, thousands of people were killed throughout Kosovo and Serbia proper.*

This is our Rule of Crisis: emergency measures are always too late. Further, we can see here an example of Machiavelli's theory of the 'misuse' of cruelty – Milosovic is driven deeper and deeper into cruelty when his hold on power unravels, as Machiavelli observes will happen if the regime is not strongly based.

The endgame unfolds with a further compounding of the fatal error, the miscalculation in Kosovo leads to domestic mistakes:

> *He had also shored up his position somewhat by creating what could (only very loosely) be called a government of national unity, bringing Vuk Draskovic, the leader of the largest opposition party … into the federal government.*

But in the end it is Draskovic who leads the last opposition wave. So we come back to the basic pragmatic rule: never build up the power of another person – in the end, Milosovic falls foul of a Machiavellian Rule of Non-appeasement.

Is Machiavelli's method of analysis, in the end, a basis for cynicism? What are the uses and the limits of Machiavellian perspectives? Here perhaps we can close with a voice from an earlier time. The Elizabethan politician and writer, Francis Bacon declared: 'we are much beholden to Machiavelli and other writers of that class, who openly and unfeignedly declare or describe what men do and not what they ought to do' (Raab, p. 74). What we gain from Machiavelli, in such contexts as the career of Milosovic, depends on how we read him – but there is a strong basis for the defence offered in the seventeenth century that he can be a source for the analysis of corruption rather than its promoter.

READING *THE PRINCE* CHAPTER IX: LUCKY JUDGEMENT – MACHIAVELLIAN CHARISMA

The Prince IX: The people's prince

IX *'On the Civil Principate'*

To counterbalance the villains, we now look at Machiavelli as a proto-theorist of democratic institutions, and democratic political success. After the self-propelled new princes, he reaches the case of the prince by popular choice, the one who does not rise through evil deeds or through violent acts, but instead ascends by the acclaim of the other citizens. This type of popular prince seems a good parallel for at least some modern democratic leaders – especially where the 'presidential' style makes the princely state seem relevant. This 'civil principate' is not a republic – the direct theme of *The Discourses* – but it is governed by a popular prince. The positive handling of this topic fits with the later work's enthusiasm for liberty, as Hulliung and others have argued. In many ways this theme corresponds to the world we inhabit in the personalized political era of the third millennium. Certainly Machiavelli's pragmatic psychology of popular success still illuminates actual events.

To begin with, Machiavelli makes a clear contrast with the preceding sections, the notorious accounts of violent transition. This structure shows Machiavelli's method of analysis: he uses a comparative approach by way of alternative scenarios. In each case, he starts with the form of the state. The state takes different forms depending on the means by which 'the prince' comes to power.

Machiavelli focuses on the politics of popularity and public opinion. Now we are in the 'civil' state, where the scale of public support dictates the rise and fall of the princes. It can appear that in such states, success is due to luck – being liked, catching the bandwagon. But for Machiavelli, those who succeed in such states possess:

KEY QUOTE

a kind of lucky shrewdness

(Norton edn, p.27)

Anatomy of key quote

o Machiavelli offers a basis for a theory of *structural luck* – which anticipates modern rational choice and game theory. There are certain situations in which some actors have luck as one of their assets.

o The theory is also a precursor of modern idea of 'charisma'. To have the quality that counts for charm is a way of possessing luck as a personality characteristic.

We will shortly see how this notion of 'lucky shrewdness' applies in relation to a contemporary example.

But first, we need to get the arguments in perspective, in order to do justice to the scope of *The Prince*. Machiavelli is famous, or notorious, for his portraits of villainy and we have seen their continuing power. But they are really an important aspect of a larger project. His deeper theme is **political rationality** and in the wider discussion he develops an underlying distinction he makes between different types or degrees of rationality.

> MODERN MACHIAVELLI
>
> *A pragmatic theory of rationality:*
> *For Machiavelli, rational politics is about different ways of responding to the specific circumstances, so as to create spaces of choice and decision.*

The villains are rational, in Machiavelli's terms, in so far as they attempt to create their own circumstances, to free themselves from the forces of chance so that they can take their own decisions. It is important to recognize that the Machiavellian villains do not generally succeed, in the long run. They eventually fall victim to the fatal error: keeping their balance is simply too difficult. The popular prince needs a different kind of rationality: the rationality of **timing**. For Machiavelli, **there is an art to being in the right place at the right time** – this art is the luck of the democratic star. The popular prince makes his luck by being in the right place at the right time: that is his 'lucky shrewdness'.

> MODERN MACHIAVELLI
>
> *Pragmatic political rationality:*
> * *Rational politics is the theory and practice of minimizing bad luck.*
> * *Politics is the art of the calculable.*

The popular prince has to be in tune with popular wishes, and this too turns out to be a source of rational judgement. You might assume that being in touch with the people is just a different kind of villainy – pandering to popular whims. In fact, Machiavelli has a rather idealistic view of the people. They are, he says, more 'honest' than other groups like aristocracies. All other factions and classes want power in order to oppress the rest of society, By contrast, the people just want to end their own oppression. There is even a link with Marxism: there is a logic in the nature of social class by which the oppressed mass would, in liberating themselves, put an end to false consciousness, the distortion of ruling classes.

There follows what can be summarized as a pragmatic rule for popular princes:

Machiavellian Rule of Popularity

The 'civil' prince is as secure as people's support for him.

If a prince comes to power through public support, he can only keep power by retaining that popularity. Such leaders are, Machiavelli implies, inclined to forget the basis of their success and suffer from delusions that they can forgo public support. They are deceived!

This sounds like a recipe for irrational decisions, but in fact Machiavelli's populace are relatively reasonable in their aims. They simply want whatever seems likely to them to reduce their own oppression and misery. This is the politics of amelioration or relative pragmatic liberation. The danger for the popular prince lies is trying to break the deal with the people. They will not sustain a ruler who seems to have betrayed them and their criterion is the reduction in their own burden.

At the end of this section on popular princedoms, Machiavelli considers responses to the decline of support, how to deal with public hostility. In a scathing analysis with continuing relevance, he exposes the use of 'emergency powers' as a self-defeating strategy. Here we have, in a different context, Machiavelli's pragmatic rule of crisis: **urgent measures are always too late**. The underlying point is that no regime can save itself by acting contrary to its own nature. If a prince came to power by public choice, he cannot survive by repressing that same public. Consequently, Machiavelli elaborates, there is no real chance of successfully turning a civil princedom into a more absolutist order. If a prince by popular support tries to take increasing power, the state is always likely to collapse. The reason is that these subjects are not resigned to accepting autocratic rulings and commands. They are accustomed to the rule of law. In other words, if there is no tradition of obeying absolutely, it will be too late to try and impose your will when things have gone wrong.

A modern popular prince

Here we see the modern form of 'lucky shrewdness', the rationality of good timing. In the UK in 1996, Tony Blair became prince by public acclaim, in a highly personalized contest that fits the Machiavellian model of the civil princedom. The scale of the success was immense (*Monthly Review*, February 1998.):

> *Commentators struggled to find words to express last year's Conservative defeat in Britain: 'wipeout', 'meltdown'.*

How had this happened? As many analysts pointed out, there was a twist to the tale. Tony Blair's New Labour had taken on board many of the policies, and also some of the key phrases, of the high tide of Conservatism under Margaret Thatcher. As a result, Blair was well placed to benefit simultaneously from continuing public support for aspects of that agenda and from equal public rejection of Mrs Thatcher's Conservative heirs, particularly in the light of ramifying allegations of 'sleaze' and a general aura of corruption. Blair benefited both from the rejection of the Conservatives and from the persistent support for elements of Conservative policy and rhetoric.

It was Tony Blair's 'lucky shrewdness' to take over just enough of his enemies' agenda at the moment when the past regime is also being rejected – so inheriting the support and benefiting from the rejection at the same instant. His was the art of being in the right ideological place at the right moment. The widely observed personal appeal of the new leader cannot – from this Machiavellian perspective – be separated from his sense of political timing.

4 Rational institutions

AIMS
In this chapter:

* We consider Machiavelli as a theorist of political institutions.

* We look at the Machiavellian view of the relationship between power and reason.

READING *THE PRINCE* CHAPTERS X–XIV: 'IT'S THE ECONOMY, STUPID' (BILL CLINTON) ... AND THE ARMY

The Prince X–XI: Measures of power

Machiavelli passes on to the more general topic of political calculation, the art of power measurement. How do you decide, he inquires, whether a state – or an institution – is strong or weak? In Machiavelli's approach, power is not defined as being obeyed so much as exercising control over one's own destiny. The opposite of power is chance. The measure of power is not whether you are obeyed all the time, but whether you decide your own course and can implement your own decisions.

Machiavelli's starting-point is that a prince is in control if he has command over the money to assemble an army – and/or the men to compose it. In other words, for Machiavelli too, 'it's the economy, stupid' – though not quite in the Clinton sense. Assembling an army is the measure of power. But this does not mean all power lies in the barrel of a gun. On the contrary, the Machiavellian question is: how do you assemble this army?

Machiavellian Measures of Political Well-being

 * *If you can pay for an army, then you must have a well-run economy in general.*
 * *If you can get volunteers, you must have a well-run and popular state and also be able to afford to fund the volunteer force.*

In other words, being able to get together an army reveals the wider basis of your power. It is the test of political rationality – and not simply a measure of how much force you can wield.

This approach is consistent with a wider vision of power politics. For Machiavelli, the stronger a regime or an institution, the more it can develop rational approaches to policy. This contrasts with the common assumption that power is naturally arbitrary. For Machiavelli, the weaker a regime, the less likely it is to develop rational policies.

How do you decide who is really in control and how much power they have? Machiavelli gives an example. Take a prince who is in command of a city. There is an enemy abroad who would like to take this power from him. But if the city is strong – if it has money and an army – and if the people support the prince – then there is no loophole for change. In such a city, there is nothing for an enemy to exploit against the status quo. The goal of rational politics is this condition of minimal bad luck. The rational state deploys public goodwill to ward off approaching bad luck. It is only a short hop from this approach to modern-day opinion research and the measurement of the strength of the state and its prince. Machiavelli lays the foundations for social science research into power – by his systematic rejection of fatalism and chance. His analysis explains why you need to know what the public thinks.

XI 'Of Ecclesiastical States'

Machiavelli turns briefly aside from these rational themes. We now have an ironic digression on supposedly perfect states, where the church has secular authority. Given Machiavelli's comments elsewhere on the role of the church, it is hard to see this section as entirely serious.

On the face of it, Machiavelli declares that when the church is also the prince, we have a perfect state. All is secure. Everyone is content, because providence and not human judgement is in command. Machiavelli adds briskly that mere mortal reason cannot comprehend such states. For Machiavelli, these theocracies *would* be the states where politics does not reach. In theory, they illustrate, by contrast, the political condition of all other states and princes. Providence is the other way to remove chance, in the shape of bad luck, from the horizon.

The Prince XII–XIV: The state and the army

As John Levitt remarked of Machiavelli in 1599, 'religion' is 'not the principall matter whereof he writeth' (Raab, p. 66). His comments are always in brackets, his concern being to define the boundaries of his true political field. Back to the real world of the state! Machiavelli next considers the military and defence aspects of the state. Here, too, his concern is with widening the space for rational policy. A strong state is one which can operate through rational policies, rather than simply the one with the biggest army.

XII 'On Different kinds of troops, especially mercenaries'

Machiavelli begins his defence analysis with a study of the conditions for failure. His reasoning takes the form: if you do not have a strong enough army, you cannot have good laws, because you cannot defend the realm of law. His focus can be seen to be on how a state breaks down.

Machiavellian First Rule of Security

If the army is weak, the law cannot be strong.

The failures of law are rooted in the lack of authority, a deficiency that in turn comes from the lack of arms. The question, then, is how to provide the military wing of the state.

Machiavelli's concern with security runs deep into his life and his diplomatic experiences, as has been traced by John Najemy in his classic study of Machiavelli's correspondence with Vettori, *Between Friends*. In this analysis of security and insecurity, Machiavelli's 'prince' becomes a representative of the human condition. As with the tragic dramatists, Machiavelli sees the predicament of the ruler as the most human condition, all too human, in the terms of Machiavelli's later admirer, Nietzsche. To be human means to be insecure, unless you create your own security. For example, no prince, Machiavelli argues, can be securely based if his state is dependent on a mercenary army. Such a prince has attempted to buy security, by paying for a ready-made force. Mercenaries are analyzed as a false path, indeed the epitome of all false pathways. You hire them to make you more secure and the result is the reverse – you end up more insecure. In fact, this is an instance of acting against your own best interests, that key theme of Machiavelli's analysis. Mercenaries have no reason to obey the prince except their pay, which is never great. This will not be sufficient in a real crisis. Nobody is going to die for a pocketful of coins, if he can avoid it!

Machiavelli here develops a philosophy of money and power. His discussion of mercenaries is at heart about capitalism and the state. How far can you base the security of your state on money?

Machiavellian Second Rule of Security

You cannot directly buy security.

That is the basis for Machiavelli's political philosophy of money. In fact, the attempt to buy security too directly rebounds. If you buy good mercenaries, you cannot really be sure of their support. Why should they let you have the benefits when they have won the battle? But if they are weak or badly run mercenaries, then you will be destroyed when they are defeated. Either way, the prospect is bad.

This is part of Machiavelli's pragmatic psychology of errors, going back to our Rule of Virtu or Risk-Taking. The more you rely on others, the weaker you will be. Machiavelli is especially fascinated by these policies because they have no conceivable good outcome. These are not even risks – they are certain disasters.

He takes the case of the famous mercenary leader, Vitelli, who was so successful that, according to this analysis, his employers had no option but to contrive his assassination! You could simply see this as classic Machiavellianism. But really the brutal outcome goes back to the original error of hiring mercenaries. The murder is the product of the false reasoning implicit in the starting-point. This example shows how bad reasoning produces violence, because that remains the only way out.

Machiavelli finds knotty paradoxes in politics as the pursuit of security. This is a predominant preoccupation of modern political strategy, and, in Machiavelli's view, this is where the prince is most likely to act against his own best interests, out of failures of political reasoning. In Machiavelli's devastating security analysis, the most common ways of pursuing security actually produce insecurity.

Here Machiavelli emerges as a modernizer, for whom past thinkers and advisers have not had a coherent theory of security. His approach to security is an application of the wider general Rule of Virtu, or Risk-Taking:

* To avoid risks is often to ensure insecurity.
* Security is on the other side of the greater risk. It is the reward for daring and for correct calculation.

XIII 'On Auxiliary troops, Mixed troops, and Your Own troops'

If you should not buy a mercenary army, then how about buying in reinforcements to help your own men? To start with, Machiavelli sounds more hopeful. Yes, you might find such reinforcements helpful. But that will only be superficial. Underneath, there will still be the makings of disaster. The same logic applies as with the mercenaries. If these auxiliaries succeed, it is their gain and not yours. If they fail, it is your failure.

This discussion of troops deepens the Machiavellian analysis of false security policy. Again, we have the key Rule of Error: the heart of false policy is weak reasoning and one moment of mistaken reasoning always cancels out a thousand advantages and right decisions. War is the area where it is most common to attribute failure to misfortune or chance. But for Machiavelli, misfortune is only one's own bad judgement in action. In particular, Machiavelli is fascinated by the adoption of policies that have no conceivable good outcome, policies such as that defined in the analysis of 'auxiliary troops'.

Machiavelli emerges here as a psychological security analyst. The terms are remote, but the logic is still alive. For Machiavelli, policy is always subject to rational analysis, in terms of your chosen goals and the likely outcomes of different course of action. He is trying to show how if you analyze many choices as policies, you discover they have no purpose at all, no coherent goal. Policy emerges, in *The Prince*, as an analytic tool. You look at the decision and ask: what are the possible outcomes? This is instead of asking other questions, such as what are the motives, the apparent reasons or what is the moral choice.

Here we reach Machiavelli's conception of political anxiety: those who grasp too eagerly for absolute security generate insecurity. The right answer is the long path, the developing of your own resources and institutions and, in particular, your own army. If the state lacks its own forces, it has no basis for security. Other supplies –

mercenaries, auxiliaries – seem like short cuts to security. In fact, they are the reverse – short cuts to disaster.

> **Machiavellian Third Rule of Security**
>
> *There is no quick fix for security.*
>
> *OR [Paradox]*
>
> *If it's easy, it won't make you secure.*

The summary is resounding:

> ## KEY QUOTE
> *I conclude, then, that unless it has its own armies, no state is really secure; in that case, it depends entirely on fortune.*
>
> (Norton edn, p.40)

Anatomy of key quote

- *'Its own armies': auxiliaries and mercenaries are the key cases of apparently reasonable decision that in fact operate against your own interests. Like Marx after him, Machiavelli is concerned to explain why men pursue actions that do not serve their true interests.*

- *'fortune': the punch-line is this idea about fortune. As Hannah Pitkin (p. 138) observes, 'Machiavelli did not invent the figure of fortune, but rather inherited it from a long tradition.' Here we can compare Machiavelli to Boethius and to medieval theories: they too sought to rescue mankind from dependence on a shifting power they called 'fortune'. Machiavellian policy is a more precise and practical means of reducing or eliminating your dependence on fortune, a long-standing philosophical goal. Thus, Machiavellian policy is taking the place of abstract virtue. Machiavelli is effectively arguing that if you want to take your life out of the hands of fortune, you need a coherent policy. In context, that is a refutation of the ideal of autonomy attained through virtue. This is a key moment where we see* The Prince *reworking an ancient tradition from within.*

In this incisive analysis of security, there has emerged a method:

MODERN MACHIAVELLI

Machiavelli's pragmatic method of policy analysis:

* *Define the decision.*

* *Think through the possible outcomes.*

* *Ask whether any of them could be regarded as a viable goal.*

* *Look at the alternative decisions and go through the same process.*

To be sure, this is not an ethical process – but neither is it anti-ethical. It is simply non-ethical.

XIV *'Military Duties of the Prince'*

Characteristically, Machiavelli then reviews defence policy from a negative point of view. If you want to lose power, he observes sarcastically, the quickest method is to pay no attention to military skills and knowledge. Make sure you have no expertise of your own as a military leader or strategist and then your power will not last long!

This is a telling observation: it is actually an example of Machiavelli's negative pragmatics of error, which one could even call his 'Rules For How to Fail' – his 'self-harm' guide for princes. One of the basic rules of political self-harm is to neglect the art of war. In fact, this is the most efficient way to defeat your own interests.

THE PRINCE CHAPTERS X–XIV APPLICATIONS:
THE RISE AND FALL OF SOUTH VIETNAM

Let us now examine how Machiavelli's treatment of security might apply to a modern example. This is one of the most notorious cases of political and security disaster: the US-backed regime in South Vietnam, focus for the Vietnam War of the 1960s and 1970s, which ended with the dramatic defeat of the Americans by North Vietnam and the collapse of the South Vietnamese state. It is this failure that has determined the course of subsequent US foreign and security policy and so helped to shape the world of the third millennium. (Our main source here is the composite US news website, psbVietnam online.)

Founding the state

South Vietnam: the beginnings

1946   France recognizes Vietnam as a 'free state', a new state, with a new prince.

1949   The Elysée agreement is signed by President Bao Dai and the French president – France promises to help create a Vietnamese anti-communist force.

South Vietnam needs an army: that is the problem with which the state is born. It is a perfect illustration of our Machiavellian First Rule of Security: without its own army, this can never be an autonomous state. Even at the beginning, the French have to stay involved in order to try and provide a force.

Hanging on to the state

Roll forward to 1964. South Vietnam is confronted by the communist North Vietnamese state.

South Vietnam: the road to disaster

1964   Lyndon Johnson wins the US election. The USA is already heavily committed to the military defence of the south. The North Vietnamese Vietcong attack an air base and this triggers a massive acceleration of American involvement.

1965   Operation 'Rolling Thunder' US bombing raids begin and last three years.

US expeditionary brigade arrive in Vietnam. US 1st Air Cavalry in action.

US troop levels top 200,000.

1967   Operation 'Cedar Falls' 16,000 US troops and 14,000 South Vietnamese advance on Saigon.

The South is clearly failing the Machiavellian test of security policy. If you haven't got the resources to take the field in your own defence, then you are lost. Any successes will belong to others and all the failures come home to you.

This is the application of our Machiavellian Third Rule of Security – if it is easy, it will not work. On the face of it, the increased US forces look like a quick fix for South Vietnam. But by applying a Machiavellian analysis, we can see behind this appearance: the paradox is at work, by which the greater the outside support, the worse the long-term insecurity of the state. The policy of the USA and the South together illustrate precisely Machiavelli's model of self-defeating strategy. The more involved the USA becomes, the less autonomous the South and the less credible it is as a sovereign state.

In this story, we are analysing **the logic of contingencies**. Machiavelli's ideas have a power to enable us to define the underlying logic connecting together scattered contingencies, apparently random or chance events.

Losing the state

As the disaster unfolds, other Machiavellian observations also apply. We see examples of his paradox of political rationality – that the only sure way to hold onto a city is to destroy it. We also see instances of his theory of misused cruelty:

South Vietnam: the start of the endgame

1968 February: Battle for Hue. 26 days of fighting by US and South Vietnamese forces eventually take Hue, but it is levelled and mass graves are revealed. Demand rises for 200,000 more soldiers. My Lai massacre. Notorious atrocity by US troops.

1969 President Nixon starts to bomb Cambodia secretly. USA declares aim of 'Vietnamization' of forces and fighting.

The fundamental theme is the one that has been present from the beginning: no army means no state, our Machiavellian First Rule of Security.

South Vietnam: the end

1974–5 South Vietnamese left to fight on their own. North advances. Khmer take Cambodia. President Ford says the war is 'finished'. South Vietnam surrenders 30 April 1975.

Here we have a pure and perfect illustration of a Machiavellian defence analysis: the perils of relying on mercenaries, and auxiliaries and outside powers. South Vietnam is a paradigm case of Machiavelli's theory of false security.

5 Moral subversion

AIMS

* Now we focus on Machiavelli's famous critique of morality – his refusal to base his advice on ethical principles.

* His apparently 'immoral' approach is seen to follow from his consistent way of explaining the autonomy of politics, the nature of political expertise.

READING *THE PRINCE* CHAPTERS XV–XIX: BEING AND APPEARANCES – THE PARADOX OF AUTHENTICITY

The Prince XV–XIX: Policy and morality

> XV 'On the reasons why men are praised or blamed – especially princes'

Under the heading of morality, the argument passes naturally to the question of the judgement of rulers and regimes. Machiavelli concentrates on explaining *why* some princes are judged positively and others are condemned. His aim is to give a coherent analysis of the logic of public opinion.

Here *The Prince* is effectively rewriting or modernizing the classical 'art' of rhetoric, the theory of persuasion. Machiavelli launches the study of 'image politics' by updating key themes from classical texts like Aristotle's *Rhetoric*. In this classical theory, praise and blame is one of the three main forms of oratory. Machiavelli wants to know more broadly how a ruler can make himself well spoken of – and avoid being the subject of abuse and vilification. It might be tempting, he implies, to pursue a good reputation by acting well. But, Machiavelli responds, since few other men are virtuous, it is unwise for the ruler to try and act virtuously all the time: he will come to no good. Again, *The Prince* counsels against the over-direct pursuit of your goal: you cannot become secure by buying defence; you cannot become well spoken of merely by being good all the time.

> Machiavellian Rule of Reputation
>
> *Since others are not good, the prince cannot benefit by being different.*
>
> **OR**
>
> *In a mixed world, good character is not the best source of a good reputation.*

By that logic, the argument reaches a famous conclusion. If the prince values reputation, he:

> KEY QUOTE
> *Must learn how not to be good.*
> (Norton edn, p. 42)

Anatomy of key quote

- *In politics, you cannot pursue your own virtue as a direct goal.* Being a good person is not a coherent policy objective. It is not that Machiavelli dismisses ethics. But he simply does not see the ruler's own virtue as the kind of goal that can be pursued through political policy. Policy is about hanging on to power – being good is a different kind of goal, an aspect of self-development under the sign of theology or morality.

- Here Machiavelli is especially *in conflict with the classical tradition* that comes from Plato's *The Republic* and the advice of Cicero. In Plato, the goal of politics is virtue – and the ruler must nurture his own virtue in order to pursue that wider goal for the citizens. Machiavelli is saying that politics cannot be the pursuit of virtue. This part of *The Prince* particularly can be seen in terms of Hulliung's view of Machiavelli as a subversive humanist – one who turns the classical tradition upside-down, from within.

o If you ask only: how can I be good, then you will fail politically. You have to ask: *how will I appear good to others?* In this context, learning not to be good means: *recognizing that you cannot pursue a good reputation by making yourself into a good person.*

o You must *recognize your own freedom, as a prince*: your freedom is greater than you thought. You can make more choices than you realized. You will only be free, if you recognize the degree of your own freedom.

Overall, this is an argument for asking the right questions. Machiavelli is a theorist of specialization – of modern reason. He is a rationalist who does not believe in the classical unity of reason, the idea that there is one way of being rational that applies to ethics and politics, theology and science. In Machiavelli's type of theory, political reason is different from ethical reason. Politics can only answer political questions, pursue political aims. Being a prince, or an adviser to a prince, is a distinct art.

This is a key moment for the historical significance of *The Prince* in the evolution of a modern concept of political life. As Hulliung puts it (p. 25), for the Machiavellian prince, 'his goodness is being good at politics, his "virtu" is virtuosity in the political arts', and this anticipates a whole modern view of society.

MODERN MACHIAVELLI

The concept of expertise:

✳ *Machiavelli breaks reason into separate arts – of which policy is one, his concern. He is developing the idea of* expertise. The Prince *is a breakthrough in the theory of what it means to be an expert and expertise is central to the development of a modern society.*

> ❋ *The expert has a special way of reasoning, fitting his own*
> *activity – policy is the form of reason appropriate to political*
> *activity. In his approach to* **specialization**, *Machiavelli*
> *foreshadows the founder of modern social theory, Max*
> *Weber, who distinguished radically different forms of human*
> *reasoning as appropriate to different forms of activity.*
> *Machiavelli's work is one of the deep roots of the sociological*
> *analysis of reason.*

In his dynamic argument, Machiavelli then goes on also to deny the unity of virtue. The virtues do not all fit together into a neat whole. A prince may well need to choose between them. And the pursuit of perfect virtue may lead to breakdown – because it simply leads towards self-contradiction, the self-defeating nature of the pursuit of ethical perfection. Yes, he concedes, everyone knows you might possess, ideally, every single good quality and nothing bad. But in fact nobody can combine all the virtues: in specific circumstances, one virtue will contradict another.

Being prudent, we might say, can rule out being generous; being courageous might prevent one being merciful. The Elizabethan poet Edmund Spenser imagined, in his epic *The Fairie Queene*, a golden chain linking every virtue. But Machiavelli sees no harmony even among the good qualities. His analysis here foreshadows the nineteenth-century philosopher Nietzsche's view of the conflict of virtues – what he called the mutual 'envy' of the virtues. In this radical argument, Machiavelli is also the precursor of the later analysis of dilemmas by contemporary thinkers like Martha Nussbaum, who distinguish practical wisdom, adapted to specific circumstances, from abstract ideals. For Machiavelli, virtue cannot be the way of resolving all our dilemmas in advance– because there are dilemmas implicit in virtue itself.

XVI *'On Liberality and Stinginess'*

We now follow the unfolding logic by which Machiavelli sees the pursuit of reputation as a key political art. Philosophically, this discussion of 'reputation' expresses a faith in the reality of appearances – do not think you can ignore or dismiss the world of appearances on behalf of some deeper realm of hidden truths and perfect virtues.

MODERN MACHIAVELLI

Image politics:

* *'Reputation' belongs to Machiavelli's upgrading of rhetorical theory: how you can persuade people to regard you. It derives from the concept of 'ethos' in classical, Aristotelean rhetoric.*

* *Reputation is also a way of thinking about the social construction of reality, to adopt a modern language. The real world – the human world – is what we make of it and what we convince others to make of it.*

* *Machiavelli argues that reputation is an appropriate goal for policy. You cannot use policy to pursue virtue, but you must use policy to pursue reputation. Reputation is also a misunderstood area of policy.*

For Machiavelli, it is a classic mistake simply to pursue the *best* possible reputation. For example, he says, it sounds fine to have a reputation for being generous. In fact, it is very dangerous to cultivate such an image, certainly by the direct route of actually *being* generous. This is a specific instance of Machiavelli's general approach, which we have termed his Rule of Reputation: to pursue a good reputation by being virtuous is self-defeating. In other words, this is another central example of Machiavelli's favourite error: the decision to take a course of action that if successful will harm you. If you aim to be thought generous, then you simply raise everyone's expectations and trap yourself in a spiral of rising hopes and demands. In fact, he adds, the wise prince will be content to have a reputation for being mean! His life will be easier. Machiavelli's view of reputation has always been a source of scandal and of misunderstanding. In the seventeenth century, a critic declared that 'Macchiavel also counseleth his prince to procure by al means to have the reputation of a religious, just and vertuous prince, though he teach him to be a most wicked tyrant' (Raab, p. 81). In fact, the analysis is far subtler and more balanced.

Here we can see just how fully developed is Machiavelli's **method of policy analysis**: work back from the possible outcomes, to decide whether this is a good decision. So if you act in such a way that you are seen as miserly, then what are the results? People have lower expectations and that serves your interests. Being mean is a vice, but it helps you stay in charge: so you are prudent if you allow your meanness to tarnish your perfect reputation. If you ask the ethical question, you conclude that meanness is a vice. But if you ask the political question, does it enable a prince to hang on, then the answer is: it is a necessary skill, an apt policy. Both answers are true – in their different contexts. Machiavelli does not deny that ethically being mean is a vice; but politically it is a skill.

KEY CONCEPT: REPUTATION

* *Machiavelli has an essentially 'rhetorical' approach to 'reputation': it is an effect of calculated persuasion, not of being good (or bad).*

* *For Machiavelli, 'reputation' is a policy tool and not an ethical goal.*

* *The prince should aim at the most useful reputation and not the most shining.*

XVIII *'On Cruelty and Clemency: Whether it is better to be loved or feared'*

As the argument unfolds, it becomes clearer what is meant by treating politics, here the arts of ruling, as a distinct field. For Machiavelli, such politics begins with the new prince, who wants to hang on to power. Hereditary rule is really pre-political. The case of the new prince makes clear how radically politics is distinct from ethics.

We now come to the dark heart of *The Prince*. Politically, one can only ask the question: does this policy help me to fulfil my objectives? If I am a new prince, then my only real objective can be to hang on to power. I cannot afford any other objectives. So the political question for the new prince is simple: does the outcome of this policy make it more or less likely that I will keep what I have won?

Machiavelli goes through some possible scenarios, his favoured approach to evaluating policies. Say, your subjects think you are cruel. That does not matter in itself, he argues – as long as the effect is to prevent trouble. If that dark reputation holds the state together, then so much the better:

KEY QUOTE

Thus, no prince should mind being called cruel for what he does to keep his subjects united and, loyal.

(Norton edn, p.45)

Anatomy of key quote: seeming bad

o This argument is about news management – how men see you must be analyzed as a practical factor, not a moral issue.

o You have to be honest with yourself about your aims. What are you trying to achieve? Then you have to ask whether your decision fits with that aim.

o **You will not achieve political success without making it your priority. Do not think you can achieve it as your secondary aim.**

The final aim is to keep control of the state – which means, of course, keeping the state together. You cannot stay in power if you neglect the coherence of the state.

From these premises, it follows that a wise prince chooses to be feared rather than loved. In Machiavelli's pragmatic psychology, the need to be loved can be a great weakness – it makes you dependent on others, when the fundamental rule is to achieve independence from the favour and resources of anyone else. This view of the need to be loved is actually consonant with some strands of contemporary psychology. Someone who needs to be loved by everyone all the time is likely to lack direction, even identity. Needing love, certainly to excess, can be a weakness and also self-defeating. In modern terms, to be dominated by the need for love may be a sign of insecurity. The same is essentially true in Machiavellian psychology. Here we meet Machiavelli as the theorist of insecurity, precursor of Freud.

Ask the pragmatic question: what are the likely outcomes of any given course of action? If you pursue a policy whose aim is to win love, you cannot expect it also to strengthen your hold on power.

Machiavellian Rule of Love And Power

To pursue love is to lose power.

The problem is that even if the policy (of winning love) succeeds, it will harm your interests. Love is a complicated emotion. Its effects on human actions are even more unpredictable and often not very reassuring. Being in love does not make people more reliable! This theme in the text has also recently been made the focus of Pitkin's feminist analysis – where Machiavelli's new approach to politics and power is seen as linked to his troubled relations with sexuality and feeling.

Machiavelli returns to the founding rule, the key to his pragmatic method. If you are 'shrewd', you will base your regime on your own resources and actions and not depend on the support of others. All dependence on other people is ultimately a way of trusting to fortune and, since fortune changes, sooner or later it will turn against you. Taking risks consists in not leaving things to chance, but acting with courage to reduce your future dependence on fortune.

Machiavelli's theory of action implies there are two kinds of risk:

* the risk that comes from *leaving* something to chance

* the risk that comes from *taking* a chance, from acting in a way which, if successful will strengthen your position. Of course, you cannot be sure of succeeding and if you fail then it may make things worse – but at least there is the possibility of a good outcome.

In line with the founding Rule of Virtu, the successful prince must be an active risk-taker, a calculator of good chances – not a passive gambler on fortune. Your approach to reputation follows: you must use it as a tool, not depend passively on the views of others.

| XVIII *'The way princes should keep their word'* |

Machiavelli now treats the question of political ways of using language. This is his further updating of the rhetorical tradition. Politics is applied rhetoric, the art of using words to achieve your own goals.

First, there is one specific use of language or, in modern terms, one kind of speech act: promising. Machiavelli is firm and we can formulate from his detached analysis our:

Machiavellian Pragmatic Rule of Speech

The fewer promises you keep, the better.

OR

Political discourse is indirect.

For Machiavelli, a promise is the most transparent possible use of words: it means what it says and says what it means and lasts into the future. He is not in favour of such transparency, for princes. This argument is about the difference between a policy and a promise. Both address the future. Consider the distinction from the perspective of modern electoral politics! To make a promise merely lays you open to inevitable accusations of betrayal; to present a policy keeps open your options, it can be reinterpreted in changing circumstances, and does not give away all your aims in one statement.

For Machiavelli's prince, language is a medium of persuasion – not of contract-making. The oblique use of words is a definitive political skill – and as such it is interestingly comparable with literary talent. The true prince should contain in his nature the 'fox' as well as the 'lion' – he must be able to speak sideways, as well as act directly.

Summing up, Machiavelli concludes that you *should* if possible seem a good person – full of mercy, kindness, honesty and so on – and even be so. But you may at any moment need to cast free of those virtuous limitations. You must not let either the substance or the appearance of virtue stand in your way.

XIX *'On avoiding contempt and hatred'* Machiavelli now clarifies his negative principle of image politics. The main aim of the prince is not to appear fine, being loathed or ridiculed. In practice, this principle does smuggle back into the discussion a slice of ethical considerations. In so far as other people view you through the lens of morality, you cannot afford to violate their expectations too abruptly. There are good, pragmatic reasons for not letting people despise you. If they respect you, people are unlikely to plot against you. Few admirers will join any conspiracy. Therefore, for example, a modern-day politician should avoid the hint of 'sleaze' – because it makes you vulnerable. And so with being hated, except that here Machiavelli adds a twist. Don't forget that people may hate you for doing good deeds, as much as for bad ones. For example, he elaborates, if everyone else is corrupt, an upright prince will simply be hated! You must tailor your reputation to the attitudes of the powerful groups in your state. If you need to cultivate the favour of the army, you must appear their kind of man, and indeed act in their kind of way. That, says Machiavelli, was the old-fashioned way; the more modern way, he adds, is to win the favour of the public in general, which will involve a very different approach to both image and action.

MODERN MACHIAVELLI

Machiavelli and philosophy:

* *In modern philosophical terms, Machiavelli's argument denies that morality is the 'metalanguage' of politics – and personal life, art and every other field of human activity. It is not that Machiavelli is a disciple of immorality; he does not believe that 'crime pays'. But he does believe that politics is a distinct art, whose focus is policy, rather than morality.*

* *At this point, we can also place Machiavelli's philosophy more broadly in context. His approach is also all about 'appearances': he can be seen as a 'phenomenalist'. Machiavelli is one of those thinkers for whom appearances are real, like Nietzsche and Sartre and as against Kant and Plato.*

THE PRINCE CHAPTERS XV–XIX APPLICATIONS: TOO MUCH OF A GOOD THING?

We now turn, in line with the traditions of Machiavelli's interpreters, to a current example to explore this observation that 'apparent kindness can turn out to be cruel … that the conventional keeping of faith can be a betrayal of public trust', in the terms of Hannah Pitkin's reading.

The story of Mikhail Gorbachev: the last good man

Mikhail Gorbachev was one of the most important political figures of the twentieth century. He was the last General Secretary of the Soviet Communist Party and the final prince to rule the Soviet Union, presiding over its dissolution and replacement in 1991 by a multitude of separate states. (Key source: CNN profile.)

Gorbachev: the rise to power:

* Born 1931 of humble origins.

* Qualified as a lawyer.

* Rise through the Communist Party Central Committee 1971.

* Secretary 1978.

* General Secretary 1985–91.

From a Machiavellian perspective, Gorbachev is on the cusp between hereditary communist rule and the new state, new prince scenario. Under the old hereditary rule, the prince is obeyed because it is the same ruling family or party. But that is coming to an end and he has to play the role of the new prince trying to make a new state.

Gorbachev was in power for six years, as one of the two most powerful people in the world, and in historic terms one of the most significant. Yet in 1991 he falls suddenly and there ensues the disappearance of the state – that is even worse than the fall of the individual prince. In general, his career is an example that goes back to the Rule of Opportunity – new states will be unstable, if you can win power, then you can lose it.

We then bring in the Machiavellian Rule of Reputation. Yes, it would be nice to seem (and be!) likeable, merciful and generous. But you cannot afford to earn such a reputation by being so all the time. In his career, it might be argued, Gorbachev does not grasp this rule. He hopes that being good will do the trick.

The good image:

'Gorbachev's leadership style proved to be a significant departure from that of past Soviet leaders. He lacked the menacing, often brutish appearance ... Gorbachev was charming, personable and intelligent. He enjoyed public appearances, and was seen frequently on television talking to Soviet citizens.'

So far, so good: it is better to seem merciful and benign. But Machiavelli also warns that if you try too hard to seem virtuous, you will only alienate people who know they are not so good themselves.

In other words, Gorbachev pursues the politics of virtue. He tries to be what he seems: he looks relaxed and he then seeks to enact a more relaxed approach. But this is taken as an invitation by rivals and enemies. As Thomas Nashe saw in the England of the sixteenth century, there is a bitter truth in Machiavelli's insight that '"new good turnes" will not "roote out old grudges"' (Raab, p. 62). The old enemies move into the vacuum. A good reputation, founded on decency, is not enough; in certain circumstances it seems even to be counterproductive.

Gorbachev: the endgame:

'Gorbachev made moves to share power with the Soviet republics, but the actions brought an attempt by hardliners to depose him in a coup.'

'Supported by Boris Yeltsin and other reformers, he resigned from the communist party. Gorbachev's further attempts to share power with the republics were to no avail ... He resigned on December 25th 1991.'

Gorbachev does not allow for the mixed emotions and motives of men generally. And, in this blurred state of mind, he makes the central error of building up his rivals, falling foul of the Machiavellian Rule of Non-appeasement.

Gorbachev's fate stands as a modern-day Machiavellian parable of 'The fall of the good man':

Since that time, he has been blamed by many Russians for their current political and economic predicament.

Here he is a classic example of the Machiavellian Rule of Reputation: that it is dangerous to appear better than other men. You may well arouse greater hatred by being fair and just than by being as corrupt as the rest.

Let's now zoom in on the coup which really brought Gorbachev's endgame to a finish. In December 1989, Gorbachev tells US President Bush that 'We don't consider you an enemy any more' and that he wishes the USA to remain a force in Europe. Here is a man trying to act well and to appear good too. He is gaining a reputation for all kinds of generosity – and that is dangerous. In the immediate aftermath of this friendly declaration, the constituent parts of Gorbachev's Soviet state begin to break up.

In May 1990, the powerful Boris Yeltsin becomes parliamentary leader of the Russian republic and 1990 ends with Gorbachev trying to preserve the USSR as a state. He fails: in April 1991 Georgia declares independence and the floodgates have opened. Then on 18 August 1991, Gorbachev is on holiday when there is an army coup. He is put under house arrest. Next day tanks enter Moscow. But Yeltsin famously resists, climbing onto a tank in Red Square, before the world's media. The coup leaders back down and 22 August Gorbachev returns, but he is finished. The state dissolves and he fades into oblivion. In Machiavellian terms, he has paid the price for pursuing a good reputation by acting well – and failing to see that such a reputation is at best a mixed blessing in a mixed world. If he had – Machiavelli might say – learnt how not to be good at times, he might have done more good in the long run.

6 Practicalities

AIMS

We see how *The Prince* focuses, in the late sections, on the dilemmas of its own time and place. But far from becoming less relevant, this practical concern is precisely the source of the book's continuing significance.

READING *THE PRINCE* CHAPTERS XX–XVI: SECURITY PARADOXES

The Prince XX–XXIII: Guidelines

> XX 'Whether building fortresses and other defensive policies often adopted by princes are useful or not'

Turning to practicalities, Machiavelli reviews some of the fashions of his own age, starting with giant castle-building projects. Castles may be out of fashion now, but massive defence and security investments are not. We can still look from Machiavelli's perspective at those forms of public expenditure whose purpose is to hold onto power over the state. For instance, a modern-day castle might be the plan introduced in 2001 for a US 'Defence Shield'. Machiavelli is neither for nor against such projects in general. But as a policy analyst, he demands a precise justification for any such investment: how will it attain its specific goal?

In this context, Machiavelli deepens his analysis of the demand for security that defeats itself. He alerts us to the political paradoxes of insecurity. Leaving behind physical projects, he turns to more abstract areas of policy. In particular, he goes on to develop the pragmatic guideline that the prince should not weaken parts of his own state. There are a number of situations in which a prince might be tempted by such a course of action. For example, says Machiavelli, take a prince who has come to power after an unstable period. There are weapons on every side: should he not begin by disarming everyone? Not at all! If he pursues disarmament, the new prince merely annoys his new subjects, without succeeding in his goals, which are impossible in any case. Better to leave the citizens armed and win their support in other ways.

Machiavellian Policy Guideline

Disarmament destabilizes the new state.

Such a guideline still seems relevant to situations where there is an attempt made to end a period of conflict, as in Northern Ireland or the Middle East. Machiavelli would see disarmament as a false path to security – too much of a quick fix, that is inevitably going to rebound.

A second pragmatic guideline follows. Despite his reputation for political cynicism, Machiavelli emerges as a critic of the politics of 'divide and rule'. You cannot strengthen your power by dividing your subjects.

Machiavellian Policy Guideline

A divided state is always less stable: divide and rule is self-defeating.

The best source of security is unity and consensus, not fragmentation and instability. Here, too, the policy approach still seems pertinent. In the modern Middle East, for instance, Israeli interests seemed to be served by fragmenting the other side, but in practice the ensuing conflict has damaged everyone and weakened rather than strengthened the state.

XXI *'How a Prince should act to acquire Reputation'*

In this practical vein, Machiavelli now defines more carefully the political paradoxes of prudence. Here he takes another stand against conventional wisdom, the wisdom of staying out of a conflict.

Take, he speculates, a classic policy dilemma. You are a relatively small state, with two neighbours who are rivals. They go to war: what is your safest course of action? On the face of things, it would be most prudent to remain neutral. But, in fact, says Machiavelli, your best policy is to side with whichever appears the stronger and hope that they win. If you stay neutral, whoever is the victor will treat you as if you were an enemy and the loser will take comfort from your misery. Stay out and keep safe? On the contrary, we can formulate the following guideline:

Machiavellian Policy Guideline

Commitment is safer than neutrality.

OR

Nobody's friend is everybody's enemy.

Negatively, this argument is designed to expose the fallacy of neutrality – nothing is less safe than staying out of the fight. Machiavelli's view of neutrality is: to be neutral is to have no friends. In 1540, this advice rang true to one English writer (Raab, p. 49) who recommended to his readers 'the proverbe of Makiavelly, which seyth that whan dawnger of a warre is over oon it is better to preven [confront] it than to defaarre it'. So, in our day, in the case of the newly independent state of Georgia in 1999, we can see this Machiavellian logic in action. There is a war between the giant Russian Federation and the break-away republic of Chechnya. At first the Georgians try to stay neutral, but that policy does not last, as the journal *Transitions* records:

Russian helicopters rained missiles on the Georgian side of the border … The Georgian resisted Moscow's main request to station troops on its side of the border, but by the end of November, President Shevardnadze had announced that Russia's war effort was justifiable and that Georgia would continue to 'conduct a relentless struggle' against Chechen terrorists.

Policy analysts conclude, exactly in tune with the Machiavellian guideline:

Though not a popular policy, conceding to Russian security concerns may in the long run prove to be more productive than a long and painful struggle to achieve total military independence.

> XXII *'On a Prince's private counsellors'*

In his catalogue of practical wisdom, Machiavelli comes to the problem of hiring and firing advisers. Here he turns out to be against the commonplace wisdom of hiring the tough guy for the rough job. On the contrary, if the candidate is a tough nut, always with an eye on his own interests, he will not be reliable.

Machiavellian Policy Guideline

Never hire an adviser who is more ruthless than you are.

The prince should not hire those who apply to themselves the rules reserved for him! This guideline can be used to explain the common falling out of political allies after they have succeeded. For example, in the UK Prime Minister, Tony Blair, sacked – twice in fact – his closest ally, Peter Mandelson. True, this was under public and political pressure. But it also fits with the Machiavellian guideline. Don't let yourself be advised by people who are pursuing their interests as ruthlessly as you must pursue yours.

> XXIII *'How to avoid flatterers'*

Next, following the theme of advice, the Prince is told that he cannot always seek to hear good news about himself. On the other hand, he must not be too open to everybody's opinions. Yes, concedes Machiavelli, you do need a reputation for listening to unpleasant truths, otherwise there is a danger that you will not find out what is going on. But you must only listen when it suits you and not get the reputation for tolerating insults all the time. To accept abuse as if it were advice is to earn yourself only contempt, not admiration.

Machiavellian Policy Guideline

Listen when you choose to hear, not when advisers choose to speak.

This guideline is full of the atmosphere of a Renaissance court. Yet it has modern-day applications. One of main questions in current politics is the role of expert advice in settling political questions. This is true across the range from military to environmental issues, from health to economics. This Machiavellian guideline suggests a general approach. Political authority must not give way to expert authority. The advice should be sought actively and not awaited passively.

The Prince XXIV–XXVI: Lucky times?

The last sections of *The Prince* close in on the surrounding scene and here we have to recall Machiavelli's own situation, recently tortured and imprisoned, seeking some kind of restoration.

XXXIV *'Why the Princes of Italy have lost their dominions'*	Machiavelli turns towards the Italian tragedy of his own times, and offers his remedy for political instability:

KEY QUOTE

The precepts given above, if properly observed, will help a new prince appear like an old one.

(Norton edn, p.66)

The aim is to help the new prince to embed his authority and the key to that goal is to create as quickly as possible the appearance of long-standing stability. You need to make your state feel natural. This surely is still the secret to many kinds of political success: that people should find it harder and harder to imagine life under other conditions. Such an approach is as relevant to democratic success as to more ruthless kinds of rule. In other words, the aim is not to generate constant excitement but, on the contrary, to exchange the intensity of the new for the reassurance of the established order as soon as possible.

A small example can be seen in the recent history of the phrase 'New Labour' in British political life. When Tony Blair won the 1996 election, his campaign relied heavily on adding the word 'new' to the old name of his party. This was designed to signal changes, but also served to generate interest and excitement. However, in the second election victory of 2001, it was mainly his opponents who were using the phrase 'New Labour' as if it were a term of abuse. The regime no longer wanted to put the emphasis on newness, but successfully exchanged that aura for the settled 'taken for granted' status of old power.

Machiavelli follows up with his diagnosis of political breakdown. If new princes lose power, it is because they have failed to observe the rules that could have converted their novelty into an established matter of fact.

XXV 'The Influence of Luck on Human Affairs and the ways to counter it'

The finale is urgent, both personally and politically. Machiavelli needs the future to begin now, with a vista of restoration. At the same time, in invoking this hope, he is also defining one of the major political problems of modern times. Once the situation has become unstable, how can stability ever be re-established? His key distinction here is between maintaining a stable state, and recreating stability from chaos. In this context, he emerges as a philosopher of human freedom, a critic of the style of fatalism that becomes popular in times of upheaval. People may prefer to see events as being beyond their control. It is common to regard the world as ruled by fortune or chance: either things are inevitable or they occur at random. It comes to the same thing – neither allows scope for free will and decisive action.

For Machiavelli, politics is the means of reasserting human judgement in the face of chaos and crisis. Yes, fortune rules half of the world; but we have power over the other half. He ends with a rich (and ambiguous) image, the last of his evocations of fortune, which as Pitkin (p. 143) shows has been the shifting centre of the whole argument in varying guises. A great river is flowing across our land. Once it is in flood, we can do nothing but wait and hope. But if we took measures in advance, we might be able to prevent the next flood, or to limit its impact. How much control, then, do we have? It is hard not to feel in this last image the strains of Machiavelli's own experience behind the traditional metaphors. How can next time be different?

In policy terms, Machiavelli's river metaphor seems to imply a threefold division: Fatalism, Grand Planning and Flexible Policy. Fatalism means just watching and hoping for the best: it involves an overreliance on fortune. Grand Planning is a modern way of defining the attitude which overestimates human mastery of our circumstances. We cannot remove the river altogether, or control the rainfall, in this metaphor. Machiavelli is the advocate of political reasoning in the third of these forms – Flexible Policy. In his concluding view, we must *adapt* to the times if we wish to survive and succeed – as princes, and perhaps as human beings generally.

XXVI '*An Exhortation to Restore Italy to Liberty and free her from the barbarians*' The book ends with a flourish that some have seen as Machiavelli's idealism. He declares that Italy awaits her new prince. But arguably, for *The Prince*, the hour is always ready for those who can define their goals in terms of a coherent policy.

Conclusion: influences, images and interpretations

MACHIAVELLI'S AFTER-IMAGES

The Prince remains one of the great riddles of intellectual history, contested by widely divergent traditions of interpretation.

In Machiavelli's case, demonization and influence have gone together:

The reception of Machiavelli:

1559   Machiavelli placed on papal index – banned by the Catholic Church.

1589   Marlowe's *The Jew of Malta* popularizes 'the murderous Machiavel'.

1611   John Donne's dialogue between Loyola and Machiavelli, featuring the demonic stereotype.

1640   *The Prince* published in English.

1640   Louis Machon was asked by Cardinal Richelieu to write an 'Apology for Machiavelli'.

1713   Michael Lilienthal's *On Literary Machiavellism* was able to treat the demonic Machiavelli as an established fact.

1762   Rousseau in *Social Contract* reads *The Prince* as a great work of republican political theory.

1801–2 Hegel, in his lectures on philosophy of history, sees Machiavelli as a world historical figure in the evolution of thought. This is the account that opens up Machiavelli to be a future influence on major modern thinkers.

(Key source: Robert M. Adams, 'The Rise, Proliferation and Degradation of Machiavellianism')

The case of the English Machiavelli is representative. Thomas
Cromwell, minister of Henry VIII, was recommending *The Prince* in
1528 (Raab, p. 32), as a practical guide. His correspondent, Reginald
Pole said it 'had already poisoned England and would poison all
Christendom'. This negative recoil grew. For example, Roger Ascham
in 1551 lamented, with *The Prince* in mind, 'Ye see what manners and
doctrine our Englishe men fetch out of Italie' (*ibid.*, p. 33). In 1572, a
political tract refers vividly to 'the hazard of turning one of the most
principal and Auncient Monarchies of Christendome, from a most
Christian Government into a Machiavellian State' (*ibid.*, p. 60).

But there was always a counter-current of affirmation. In the mid-
seventeenth century, Clarendon (Raab, p. 151) declared of
Machiavelli that 'he was as great an enemy to tyranny and injustice
in any government as any man then was or now is'. He was a realist,
not a cynic, in this analysis.

The ambiguous story continues into modern times. Thinkers such as
the Italian Croce and the French existentialist Merleau-Ponty have
struggled to reconcile Machiavelli's interest in power with a more
liberal or even socialist ethos (Hulliung, p. 7). Debate has continued
among recent interpreters and commentators. Their arguments
mirror the ambiguous history, the ambiguous lineage of
Machiavellianism. On the one hand, there is **the pragmatic Prince**,
Machiavelli as the origin of grown-up policy-making:

> *If politics be thought of as the art of dealing with the
> contingent event, it is the art of dealing with fortuna as the
> force which directs such events ... contingency.*
>
> (Pocock, p.156)

In this analysis, Machiavelli is the founding analyst of 'the ruler as
innovator' (*ibid.*, p. 156). This sense of Machiavelli's pragmatism has
been a central strand in our guided reading.

But then there is what can be termed **the Utopian Prince**. Here *The Prince* appears as a great argument for human freedom and responsibility, as in the approach initiated by Felix Gilbert. In this analysis, Machiavelli's apparent cynicism is the flip side of a recognition of political free will: 'political action cannot be kept within the limits of morality' because it has no fixed limits beyond those which we choose to give it. This is not an easy utopianism or idealism to digest, though. In such approaches, *The Prince* is an expression of an ideal, though with a dark side:

> *Machiavelli believed in the creative power of man in the world of politics.*
>
> ('Fortune, necessity, virtu', reprinted in Norton edn)

J. R. Hale in his *Machiavelli and Renaissance Italy* saw *The Prince* as appearing within the established theories 'like a bomb in a prayerbook'. Our reading is also coloured by this fraught but affirmative tradition of interpretation.

But then, as against both of these perspectives, we must also bear in mind the contrasting point of view, which might be called **the Totalitarian Prince**:

> *That Machiavelli's Prince contains the most immoral things and that Machiavelli has no scruples about recommending to the ruler all sorts of deceptions, of perfidy, and cruelty is incontestable.*
>
> (Ernst Cassirer, 'Implications of the new theory of the state', reprinted in Norton edn)

OVERVIEW

The Prince is many things. It is a great work of literature, as well as philosophy and history. The book depends on its author's power of weaving sharp stories into his arguments at each stage. Then again, the book is a work of practical advice or appears to be. As a self-help guide for Renaissance rulers, *The Prince* might be expected to have become redundant. But its positive prescriptions are derived by looking at what has gone wrong in actual cases or plausible cases; and this negative analysis remains devastatingly applicable.

Machiavelli's deep pragmatism is such that it is hard to understand except through thinking about particular situations. He has a specific and unusual type of wisdom to offer – a practical wisdom, limited but with the power to illuminate many dark corners of history. In this guide, for instance, we have focused on the career of Slobodan Milosovic, the Serbian ruler in the 1990s, and the rise and fall of Mikhail Gorbachev, one-time hero in the 'reform' of the Soviet Union in the 1980s. We have also seen that the arguments have democratic application, for example to the case of the UK leader, Tony Blair. Machiavelli's distinctive contribution is to have made it plausible that we can understand these great stories of rise and, in the end, fall – rationally, analytically but also in individual and psychologically plausible terms and with some hope of practical advice or remedy. It is Machiavelli's pragmatic understanding of the relation between success and failure that makes the book so rich.

REFERENCES AND FURTHER READING

A lively and accessible biography, which is also a key source for the biographical sections:
Maurizio Viroli, *Niccolo's Smile: A Biography of Machiavelli* , trans. by Antony Shugaar (Farrar, Straus and Giroux, 2000).

Another lively introduction:
Quentin Skinner, *Machiavelli: A Very Short Introduction* (Oxford University Press, 1981).

Key critical articles reprinted in the Norton edition include:
Isaiah Berlin, 'The question of Machiavelli'; Felix Gilbert, 'Fortune, necessity, virtu'; Ernst Cassirer, 'Implications of the new theory'; J. R. Hale, 'Machiavelli and Renaissance Italy'.

Some important studies of Machiavelli's life and thought:
Mark Hulliung, *Citizen Machiavelli* (Princeton University Press, 1983).
John M. Najemy, *Between Friends: Discourses of Power and Desire in the Machiavelli-Vettori Letters of 1513–15* (Princeton University Press, 1993).
Hannah Fenichel Pitkin, *Fortune is a Woman: Gender and Politics in the Thought of Niccolo Machiavelli* (University of California Press, 1984).

On the influence of Machiavelli, a lively study is:
Felix Raab, *The English Face of Machiavelli* (Routledge and Kegan Paul, 1965).
Another account is that of Robert M. Adams, reprinted in the Norton edition as 'The rise, proliferation and degradation of Machiavellianism'.

Key study of context:
J. G. A. Pocock, *The Machiavellian Moment* (Princeton University Press, 1975).

A lively contextual narrative:
Christopher Hibbert, *The Rise and fall of the House of Medici* (Penguin, 1979).

A major source:
Machiavelli and His Friends: Their Personal Correspondence, translated and edited by James B. Atkinson and David Sices (Northern Illinois University Press, 1996), which contains helpful outlines as well as gripping letters referred to in the biographical section.

There is a Penguin edition of Machiavelli's *The Discourses*.

INDEX